Gay & Lesbian HISTORY FOR KIDS

Gay & Lesbian HISTORY FOR KIDS

The Century-Long Struggle for LGBT Rights

WITH **21** ACTIVITIES

JEROME POHLEN

CHICAGO REVIEW PRESS

Copyright © 2016 by Jerome Pohlen
First edition
Published by Chicago Review Press, Incorporated
814 North Franklin Street
Chicago, Illinois 60610
ISBN 978-1-61373-082-9

Library of Congress Cataloging-in-Publication Data
Pohlen, Jerome.
 Gay and lesbian history for kids : the century-long struggle for LGBT rights, with 21 activities / by Jerome Pohlen. —
First edition.
      pages cm. — (For kids)
 Includes bibliographical references and index.
 ISBN 978-1-61373-082-9 (trade paper)
 1. Gay rights—United States—History—Juvenile literature. 2. Gays—United States—History—Juvenile literature. I. Title.

HQ76.8.U5P64 2015
323.3′2640973—dc23

                                                                                              2015010563

Cover and interior design: Monica Baziuk
Interior illustrations: James Spence
Cover images: Front cover (from left): Rainbow flag, © Alexander Demyanenko/Shutterstock; Harvey Milk, Photo
© Pat Rocco, all rights reserved; Gay Liberation Front, Photo by Diana Davies, Manuscripts and Archives Division, The
New York Public Library; Julie, Annie, and Hillary Goodridge, © Jessica Rinaldi/Reuters/Corbis; Oscar Wilde, Library
of Congress (LC-USZC4-7095); Stonewall Inn, Photo by Diana Davies, Manuscripts and Archives Division, The New
York Public Library; Keith Haring ACT UP poster, ACT UP New York Records, Manuscripts and Archives Division,
The New York Public Library, Astor, Lenox, and Tilden Foundations, © Keith Haring Foundation; We'wha, National
Anthropological Archives, Smithsonian Institution (02440800); Out and Proud pin, author's collection. Back cover image of
the White House by Ted Eytan.
The Equality Logo on page 77 is a registered trademark of the Human Rights Campaign. It has been reproduced in this book
with the permission of the Human Rights Campaign.

Printed in the United States
5 4 3 2 1

For my mother, Barbara Jean Standiford Pohlen,

who taught me about empathy and compassion

Contents

Time Line

570 BC Greek poet Sappho dies

1503–06 Leonardo da Vinci paints the *Mona Lisa*

1855 Walt Whitman publishes *Leaves of Grass*

1871 Germany enacts Paragraph 175

1895 Oscar Wilde goes on trial in London

1897 Magnus Hirschfeld founds the Scientific-Humanitarian Committee in Germany

1924 Henry O establishes the Society for Human Rights in Chicago

1930 Lili Elbe undergoes the first sex-reassignment surgery in Berlin

1945 World War II veterans establish the Veterans Benevolent Association

1950 Friends found the Mattachine Society in Los Angeles

1952 Christine Jorgensen becomes America's most famous transgender person

1955 The Daughters of Bilitis is founded in San Francisco

1956 Dr. Evelyn Hooker releases her groundbreaking study on gay men

1965 LGBT activists picket the White House at the first Annual Reminder

1969 Stonewall Uprising erupts

Gay Liberation Front is founded

Gay Activist Alliance is founded

1970 Lavender Menace and Radicalesbians are founded

1973	Jeanne and Jules Manford establish PFLAG
	Homosexuality is removed as a mental illness from the *DSM*
1977	Anita Bryant's Save Our Children campaign targets Miami
	Harvey Milk is elected to San Francisco's Board of Supervisors
1978	Gilbert Baker designs the first rainbow flag
	Harvey Milk and San Francisco mayor George Moscone are assassinated
1979	First National March on Washington for Lesbian and Gay Rights is held
1981	AIDS is first reported in the *New York Times*
	Larry Kramer and friends establish the Gay Men's Health Crisis in New York
1982	First Gay Games are held in San Francisco
1986	Supreme Court issues *Bowers v. Hardwick* decision
1987	ACT UP is founded in New York
	Second National March on Washington for Lesbian and Gay Rights is held
1989	Denmark offers first "registered partnerships" to same-sex couples
1993	Third March on Washington for Lesbian, Gay, and Bi Equal Rights & Liberation is held
	"Don't Ask, Don't Tell" is signed by President Clinton

1996	"AIDS cocktail" is first introduced
	Defense of Marriage Act is passed and signed by President Clinton
1997	Ellen DeGeneres comes out
1998	Matthew Shepard is murdered in Laramie, Wyoming
2000	Vermont offers "civil unions" to same-sex couples
2003	Supreme Court overturns *Bowers* decision with ruling in *Lawrence v. Texas*
	Massachusetts Supreme Court strikes down same-sex marriage ban
2004	San Francisco "Winter of Love" is launched by Mayor Gavin Newsom
2005	Canada makes same-sex marriage legal nationwide
2008	California Supreme Court strikes down state marriage ban
	Proposition 8 passes in California, halting same-sex marriages
2009	President Obama signs the Matthew Shepard and James Byrd Jr. Hate Crimes Prevention Act
2010	Dan Savage and Terry Miller launch the It Gets Better Project
	Don't Ask, Don't Tell is repealed, effective in 2011
2012	President Obama becomes first US president to support full marriage equality
2013	Supreme Court strikes down Defense of Marriage Act
2015	Supreme Court rules in *Obergefell v. Hodges* that same sex marriage is legal nationwide

Two Moms

"**Hold on a minute!**" the hospital worker said, holding up her hands. "There can't be two moms in there."

What? Theresa Volpe was stunned. She had just raced to the hospital in an ambulance with her son Jaidon, who was dying from kidney failure. Volpe's partner, Mercedes Santos, had followed in their car. But in the chaos of the emergency room, Mercedes ended up inside the pediatric intensive care unit with Jaidon, while Theresa was outside the unit's entrance, pleading with a hospital worker who wouldn't let her pass. To keep track of who was in the unit, Mercedes had been given a "Mother" wristband, and all that was left was a "Father" wristband.

"Are you the stepmother?" the worker asked. "We can let you in if you're the stepmother."

No no no no no, Theresa thought, *this isn't happening*. She quickly called Mercedes on her cell phone. As much as she hated to leave Jaidon's side, Mercedes rushed out to get Theresa, leaving her 18-month-old son with the doctors trying to save his life. Soon they were both arguing with the hospital worker, and getting nowhere.

Theresa and Mercedes had been a couple for 19 years. They'd built a home and business together, and were now raising two children—Ava and Jaidon. But they didn't have time to explain any further. At this moment, only one thing mattered: Jaidon needed his mothers.

▼ ▲ ▼

THIS CONFRONTATION DID not happen decades ago in a hospital that had never seen lesbian parents. This happened in Chicago. In 2011. There was no excuse for the way their family was being treated.

The long, difficult struggle for lesbian, gay, bisexual, and transgender (LGBT) rights is filled with stories of people like Theresa and Mercedes who stood up against injustice, often after they experienced it first-hand. What happened in the hospital that day would later change the hearts of many, and eventually change laws in the state of Illinois. Theresa, Mercedes, Ava, and Jaidon would follow in a grand tradition that started more than a century ago and continues to this day.

But before you learn what they did, it's important to understand how they, and all of us, got to this point.

© Braden Gunem

"And crown thy good with brotherhood,
from sea to shining sea!"

—Katharine Lee Bates

A Brief History

to 1900

July 22, 1893 ▶ The group of professors started in a horse-drawn prairie wagon early in the morning. Halfway to the summit of Pikes Peak the drivers switched to mules, which were better in the thin air. When the wagon reached the top, everyone got out to take in the view. At 14,115 feet above sea level, it seemed as if they could see from one ocean to the other.

Katharine Lee Bates was overcome with emotion. "It was then and there, as I was looking out over the sea-like expanse of fertile country spreading away so far under those ample skies, that the opening lines of the hymn floated into my mind," she later recalled.

O beautiful for halcyon skies . . .

The rest of the words would come later. But before she headed back from the mountaintop, Bates sent a telegram to her mother back home: "Greetings from Pikes Peak, gloriously dizzy. Wish you were here."

◀ **Pikes Peak as seen from Garden of the Gods, circa 1900.** Library of Congress (LC-DIG-ppmsca-17814)

Katharine Lee Bates, circa 1885.

Though Bates's mother was not with her that day, Katharine Coman was. The pair had traveled together from back east, invited to be guest lecturers at Colorado College. On the journey west, their train rolled through Kansas on July 4, where they watched wheat fields blowing in the summer breeze. Bates wrote in her diary that she was "A better American for such a Fourth."

The memories of that summer trip with Coman would one day become a poem titled "America." The poem would later be set to music by Samuel Augustus Ward and become the song you know today, "America the Beautiful."

> *O beautiful for spacious skies,*
> *For amber waves of grain,*
> *For purple mountain majesties*
> *Above the fruited plain.*
> *America! America!*
> *God shed His grace on thee,*
> *And crown thy good with brotherhood*
> *From sea to shining sea.*

▼ ▲ ▼

How Do We Know?

NOBODY HAS ever proven that Katharine Lee Bates and Katharine Coman were lesbian. "The Professors Katharine," as they were known around Wellesley College, were certainly close. For 25 years they lived together in a "Boston marriage," a popular term used to describe two unmarried women who depended on one another emotionally and behaved much like a married couple.

And they definitely were a couple. The two had met at Wellesley in 1887. Coman taught history and economics; Bates was the head of the English department. Starting in 1894, the women shared a home and never separated until Coman died in 1915. After Coman's death, Bates published a collection of poems for her lost partner titled *Yellow Clover*, where she called their relationship "one soul together."

The further back in history you look, the more difficult it is to know who was and wasn't lesbian, gay, bisexual, or transgender. The issue wasn't discussed often, and if it was discussed, it was usually in a negative way. (The words *homosexual* and *heterosexual* didn't even exist before 1868.) Years ago most personal relationships—marriages, families, friendships—were very different than they are today. Bates and Coman might not have even thought of themselves as lesbian, just different.

Despite this, it doesn't make sense to assume everyone in history was heterosexual until proven otherwise. Most people have dark hair—does that mean you should assume everyone in history has had dark hair unless described as another color? Given what we know of Bates, Coman, and their lives together, doesn't it make more sense to say they probably were *lesbian* unless proven otherwise?

As you will soon learn, history is filled with lesbian, gay, bisexual, and transgender people. We know this through rare published histories, personal letters, court transcripts, and other sources. For years, much of this history was hidden, ignored, or erased by those who would rather not discuss it. But it is a fascinating, rich history, and our world would not be the same without the contributions of the LGBT community, invisible or not.

Homosexuality Through the Centuries

FOR AS long as there has been human civilization, LGBT people have played a part—from farmers to poets, generals to foot soldiers, peasants to queens and kings. In some cultures, same-sex couples and transgender persons were accepted as part of everyday life. But in many, they were persecuted.

Ancient Greece was comfortable with homosexuality. The Greek philosopher Socrates (circa 469–399 BC)—who told his pupils "Know thyself" and "The unexamined life is not worth living"—was gay. So was his student Plato (427–347 BC), another great philosopher. The Greek poet and composer Sappho (circa 625–circa 570 BC) wrote about love between women. She set her poems to music played on a type of harp called a lyre. Sappho ran a school for young women on the island of Lesbos. This is where the word *lesbian* comes from.

The military genius Alexander the Great (356–323 BC), born in the Greek kingdom of Macedon, established an empire that stretched from modern-day India and Afghanistan in the east to Egypt and Greece in the west. He often led his own soldiers into battle, and he

Sappho performs for an audience.
Library of Congress (LC-USZ62-120246)

FIND AQUARIUS

ACCORDING to Greek mythology, Aquarius is forever pouring water from his urn in the evening stars. Can you find it?

You'll Need

▶ Computer with Internet access and printer

▶ Binoculars or telescope (optional)

▶ Pen or pencils

In North America, the constellation Aquarius is best seen in the month of January around 9 PM. (If you stay up later, you can also see it at 10 PM in December, or 11 PM in November.) You may not be able to see it clearly from a city because of light pollution. If you can go to the country, far from the bright lights, it will be easier to find. Binoculars or a telescope will also make viewing easier.

To begin, find a star map for the January sky in your area—check www.astroviewer .com, then click "Current Night Sky" and enter your city. Print it out the day before you plan to use it, for the same hour as you will be stargazing.

Imagine a line running north to south over your head. As you look along this line, there will be a bright star, almost alone, in the southern sky. This is Fomalhaut in the constellation Piscis Austrinus—the Southern Fish. Above Fomalhaut, zigzagging down toward it, will be several dimmer stars. These represent the flow of water out of Aquarius's jar and into the mouth of the fish. Now look at your star map. Can you fill in the rest of the constellation?

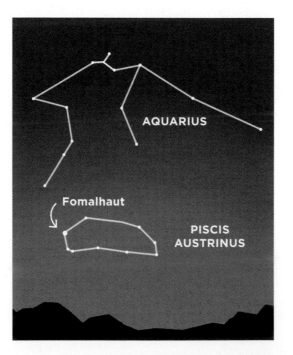

never lost in eleven years. He was also bisexual. Hephaestion, the commander of his cavalry, was his partner.

Homosexuality also appears in Greek mythology. The young mortal Ganymede so appealed to Zeus that he took him to live on Mount Olympus, where he became cupbearer to the gods. Hera became jealous, but Zeus still honored Ganymede by placing him in the night sky as the constellation Aquarius.

In ancient China, the last emperor of the Han Dynasty, Ai (27–1 BC), reportedly "did not care for women," even though he was married. He fell in love with Dong Xian, a male politician, and later named him head of the armed forces. Emperor Ai had hoped that Dong Xian would succeed him as the next emperor, but when Ai died unexpectedly, the Grand Empress Dowager Wang seized power.

In Europe and the Middle East, the Roman Empire followed the Greeks, where again, homosexuality was common, and some Roman men married one another. The emperor Hadrian (AD 76–138) was bisexual, and when his partner Antinous drowned in the Nile River, Hadrian built a city, Antinopolis, in his honor. Hadrian was considered one of the five "Good Emperors," fair and thoughtful rulers who were respected by their people. (Other Roman emperors were not so good, and even barbaric.)

Farther east, in India, sacred Hindu texts tell of gods changing their gender, or gods that were both male and female, like Lakshmina-rayan, and of same-sex divine couples giving birth to children.

Culture Connections

MUCH OF the world's art and literature has been created by LGBT individuals.

You may be familiar with *One Thousand and One Arabian Nights*, the collection of Arabic and south Asian folktales that includes stories of Sinbad the Sailor, Ali Baba, and Aladdin's lamp. One of the many contributors to the work, the Persian poet Abū Nuwās (circa 756–814), was most likely gay. Some of the tales include homosexuality, but for many years the gay passages were deliberately rewritten to disguise them.

The Italian genius Leonardo da Vinci (1452–1519), best known for his fresco of the *Last Supper* and his painting of the *Mona Lisa*, was also a brilliant scientist, and he was gay. So was Michelangelo (1475–1564), who painted the ceiling mural of the Vatican's Sistine Chapel and sculpted *David* and the *Pietà*, one of the most famous Renaissance depictions of Jesus Christ.

William Shakespeare (1564–1616) may have admitted to being bisexual in Sonnet 144. Most of his sonnets, first printed without his permission in 1609, are dedicated to "Mr. W. H." and addressed from Shakespeare to a man. When the romantic poems were published in 1640, however, many of the male pronouns were changed to female, and remained that way for another 150 years.

There have also been many gay and lesbian kings and queens throughout the centuries—James I (1566–1625) of England, namesake of the King James Bible; Christina of Sweden (1626–1689), who stepped down from the throne rather than be forced to marry; and Frederick the Great (1712–1786) of Prussia. Some of these rulers were honorable; others were downright evil. And a few were eccentric. Ludwig II of Bavaria (1845–1886) was known as "Ludwig the Mad" because he spent more time building elaborate castles than he did ruling. His famous Neuschwanstein Castle became the inspiration for Sleeping Beauty Castle at Disneyland.

Two-Spirit People

NATIVE AMERICAN culture has a long tradition of "two-spirit" people—tribal members who do not fit into standard gender roles, but instead are thought of as having a third or alternative gender. Two-spirit people have existed in more than 130 different native cultures. They were often given unique responsibilities, depending on their tribes' traditions. Some

Leonardo da Vinci and the *Mona Lisa*.

were believed to have special abilities, like predicting the weather, healing, or providing spiritual protection. Others acted as matchmakers, name givers, and marriage counselors.

"Two-spirit" is a general term used to describe people who were as different as the tribes to which they belonged. The Pawnee called two-spirits *winkte*. Zuni, *lhamana*. Navajo, *na'adlech*. Among the Mojave, two-spirits born biologically male were called *alyha*, while those born female were *hwame*. Sadly, as with so many aspects of Native American culture, the two-spirit tradition was suppressed by European colonists, Christian missionaries, and the US government, though it did not vanish entirely. Recently, the two-spirit tradition has returned to many tribes.

One of the most famous two-spirit people was a Zuni *lhamana* named We'wha (pronounced WEE-wah). Born in 1849, We'wha eventually became a leader in the pueblo (village) of *Halona:idiwana*—"The Anthill at the Middle of the World"—near the present Arizona–New Mexico border. Around age three or four, he began showing traits of a two-spirit, so he was trained in "women's tasks" such as gardening, weaving, and pottery making.

We'wha holding a clay ceremonial basket with sacred corn, 1886. National Anthropological Archives, Smithsonian Institution (02440800)

In the winter of 1885–86, anthropologist Matilda Stevenson brought We'wha to Washington, DC. He soon became the talk of the town, though most Washingtonians believed We'wha to be an Indian princess. A newspaper reported, "Society has had recently a notable addition in the shape of an Indian princess of the Zuni tribe.... Princess Wawa goes about everywhere at all of the receptions and teas of Washington wearing her native dress.... The ladies crowded about the Princess Wawa and amused themselves endlessly in attempting to converse with her by signs and broken English."

We'wha helped the Smithsonian Institution better understand Zuni culture, and demonstrated weaving on a loom set up on the National Mall. In May he participated in the society event of the season, the Kirmes, an amateur pageant held at the National Theatre. More than 280 people in traditional costumes paraded around the stage in a "gathering of the nations," and We'wha performed a traditional Zuni dance. (The charity event raised $5,000 for a local hospital.) And on June 23, 1886, We'wha presented a wedding gift to President Grover Cleveland and his new wife in the Green Room of the White House.

We'wha eventually returned to the pueblo, where he died in 1896 at the age of 49. The loss of the Zunis' much-loved leader caused "universal regret and distress."

New Worlds, Old Laws

SAD AS it is, another reason historians know that LGBT people have long existed is that laws were written to persecute them. Court records tell of LGBT people who were arrested and punished.

In 1642, two decades after the Plymouth Colony was established in Massachusetts, Edward Michell and Edward Preston were discovered together. They were put on trial and found guilty, and were publically whipped in Plymouth and again at Barnstable. In 1649, Sarah White Norman and Mary Vincent Hammon were charged with the crime of being lesbians; Plymouth authorities forced Norman to make a public confession. Transgender behavior was also outlawed in the colonies. In 1696, Massachusetts passed a law against cross-dressing.

There were, however, some positive changes in the law. In France, the Declaration of the Rights of Man was approved in 1789, at the start of the French Revolution. It proclaimed the right "to do anything that does not injure others." The declaration led to the repeal in 1791 of laws against same-sex relationships. In 1810 it was incorporated into the Napoleonic Code, which extended the same freedoms to French colonies and territories.

No other colonial empire, nor the newly established United States, did the same.

Changing Minds

THE LAWS in the newly independent United States weren't much friendlier to LGBT people than those of the colonial era. But in the 1800s many of the country's greatest minds were more open and accepting.

Famous freethinkers like Ralph Waldo Emerson (1803–1882), Henry David Thoreau (1817–1862), and Louisa May Alcott (1832–1888) all wrote about same-sex intimacy. Once, in explaining to poet Louise Chandler Moulton why she never married, Alcott admitted, "I have fallen in love with so many pretty girls and never once the least bit with any man." The works of author Herman Melville (1819–1891), including *Moby Dick*, *White-Jacket*, and his unfinished short novel *Billy Budd*, occasionally mentioned, but more often hinted at, gay life among their characters.

Emily Dickinson (1830–1886), who was influenced by the writings of Emerson, wrote passionate poetry that she mostly kept to herself—fewer than a dozen of her poems were published during her lifetime. After she died, however, more than a thousand poems were discovered in her home and were later printed. For years, they were altered—"she" and "her" turned to "he" and "him" in love poems. Dickinson's letters to her close friend Susan Gilbert were also edited by the poet's niece to make them sound less romantic.

Whether any of these men and women were gay, lesbian, or bisexual is still debated. Maybe they were just writing in the flowery, romantic style of the time. Or maybe they were trying to explore topics that weren't openly discussed. We may never know for sure. There is no debate, however, about the great American poet Walt Whitman. He was certainly gay.

General Friedrich Wilhelm von Steuben (1730–1794)

When Baron von Steuben arrived at Valley Forge on February 23, 1778, riding in a 24-belled sleigh, wearing a full-length fur coat, and holding a miniature greyhound, George Washington's soldiers were not sure what to think of him. They didn't know that he had fled Europe after accusations that he was gay. Benjamin Franklin, who had met Steuben in France, suggested that the baron should come to the United States and help with the revolution.

The Prussian-born commander quickly transformed the hungry and weary troops into a model company that turned the tide in the American Revolution. He eventually became Washington's chief of staff, and his training manual, *Regulations for the Order and Discipline of the Troops of the United States*, was used by the US Army for 30 years.

Steuben was awarded a pension and American citizenship for his service to the new nation. When he died in 1794, he willed most of his estate to his former aide-de-camp, General Benjamin Walker, and Captain William North, who had also served the baron. (Steuben never married, but both men were believed to have been partners to him at different times.) To his adopted son, John Mulligan Jr., he left his library and maps.

Library of Congress (LC-USZ61-260)

Leaves of Grass

WALT WHITMAN printed just 795 copies of the first edition of *Leaves of Grass*. It was published on July 4, 1855. The book was 95 pages long and contained only twelve poems. And yet, this slim collection would change poetry forever.

Whitman was always scribbling in a notebook, capturing his observations of America in the 1800s. Every few years he released a new, longer version of *Leaves of Grass*. The third edition came out in 1860 and included what are known as the "Calamus" poems. In them he wrote about men, together, in lifelong supportive friendships, which he called "adhesiveness." It wasn't openly gay, but it was close. For example, in "Live Oak, with Moss" he wrote:

But the two men I saw to-day on the pier, parting the parting of dear friends
The one to remain hung on the other's neck and passionately kissed him—while the one to depart tightly prest the one to remain in his arms.

During the Civil War, Whitman worked as a nurse at Union army hospitals. This led to a job as a clerk in the Department of the Interior after the war. But when the secretary of the interior learned about his Calamus poems, Whitman was fired.

Shortly after he was let go, Whitman met a man named Peter Doyle in Washington, DC. Doyle was a horse-car conductor, and Whitman was a passenger on his route. In 1895, Doyle recalled when they first met: "We were familiar at once—I put my hand on his knee—we understood.... From that time on we were the biggest sort of friends."

Probably because of the persecution he had suffered, Whitman never publicly admitted that he was gay. He made efforts to protect his private life. In his diaries, Whitman would refer to Doyle as only "16.4"—P is the 16th letter in the alphabet, and D the 4th—so "16.4" was "PD," or Peter Doyle.

Whitman suffered a stroke in January 1873, and was moved to his brother's home in New Jersey to recover. Doyle moved nearby and would visit the bedridden poet each evening before reporting for work as a brakeman on the Pennsylvania Railroad. Whitman had another stroke in 1888, and a year later the ninth and last edition of *Leaves of Grass* was printed.

Whitman died on March 26, 1892. In his will he left his pocket watch to Peter Doyle, "with my love." But Doyle already had something he prized even more: Whitman's old sweater. "I now and then put it on, lay down, and think I am in the old times," Doyle later wrote. "Then Walt is with me again.... It is like Aladdin's Lamp. I do not ever for a minute lose the old man. He is always nearby."

Were they or weren't they? Emerson, Thoreau, Alcott, Melville, and Dickinson.

Library of Congress (LC-USZ62-116399, LC-USZ61-361, LC-USZ61-452, LC-USZ62-135949, LC-USZ62-90564)

Walt Whitman (left) and Peter Doyle, 1865.
Library of Congress (LC-USZ62-79930)

WRITE A FREE VERSE POEM

WALT WHITMAN didn't invent the style of poetry known as "free verse," but he made it popular. Poems written in free verse do not have a set length or rhythm, and they do not rhyme. Instead, they sound more like natural speech.

It is easier to see than to explain. Take a look at the first two lines of "Paul Revere's Ride" by Henry Wadsworth Longfellow:

Listen my children and you shall hear
Of the midnight ride of Paul Revere,

Now read the opening passage of Whitman's "Song of the Open Road," from *Leaves of Grass*:

© awrangler

Afoot and light-hearted, I take to the open road,

Healthy, free, the world before me,
The long brown path before me lead-ing wherever I choose.

The difference is immediately clear. And while there appear to be no rules in free verse, these poems have some things in common. Free verse usually paints a vivid "word picture" that expresses feel-ings and emotions, and words are care-fully chosen and placed. A poem about a quiet walk in the woods will sound very different than a poem about a bike ride down a steep hill.

Now it's your turn. Choose a subject for a free verse poem—something you feel strongly about, something that you can describe in detail. As you write, think about every word. Will the words make the reader *feel* what you are trying to describe?

Hiding in Plain Sight

IN THE 1800s it became easier for LGBT women and men to live the lives they wanted to live. Some left their home communities, moved to cities, joined the military, or struck out for the American West. And while it was still not pos-sible to be "out," some brave individuals built quiet lives and relationships on their own terms.

The chaos of the Civil War made it possible for some women to join the fight by enlist-ing as men. Historians have estimated that as many as 1,000 women may have done so. Most of these soldiers likely joined because they wanted to serve their country, or they needed the money, but women were not allowed to en-list. Some, like Albert Cashier, who fought in Company G of the 95th Illinois Infantry, were also probably transgender.

Born in Ireland as Jennie Irene Hodgers in 1843, Cashier was already living in America as a man when the war broke out. His unit was part of the Army of Tennessee under General Grant. Cashier was captured by the Confederates dur-ing the Siege of Vicksburg, but escaped and stayed in the army until the war ended in 1865.

After the South's surrender, Cashier re-turned to Illinois to work as a handyman. He collected a military pension and voted in elec-tions. (This was before women had that right.) In 1911 he was hit by a car, and the doctor who treated him discovered his secret. The doctor kept quiet, but when Cashier entered the Soldiers and Sailors Home in Quincy a year later, the doctor told the director of the home. The director didn't tell anyone else.

However, when Cashier moved to Watertown State Hospital in 1913, word got out. He was forced to wear a dress for the rest of his life, which wasn't long. Cashier died on October 10, 1915, and was buried in his Civil War uniform at the Sunny Slope Cemetery in Saunemin, Illinois. His headstone honored the way he saw himself: "Albert D. J. Cashier. Co. G., 95 Ill. Inf."

Cashier was not alone. Newspapers from the Old West are filled with stories of women "masquerading" or "passing" as men, and men as women. "One-eyed Charley" Parkhurst lived in Santa Cruz County, California, from the 1850s to his death in 1879, when it was discovered that he had been born female. He had worked as a stagecoach driver, lumberjack, saloon manager, and ranch hand.

Male-to-female transgender pioneers also existed. A Mexican-born woman known as Mrs. Nash worked as a laundress, cook, and midwife for the US Seventh Cavalry from 1868 to 1878, with the later years at Fort Abraham Lincoln in the Dakota Territory. She married three times. The first two soldiers deserted her, but her final husband, Sergeant John Noonan (an aide to General George Custer), was with her for the last five years of her life. When Nash lay dying of appendicitis, with her husband away on patrol, she asked that she be buried immediately in the clothes she wore. Her friends did not follow her wishes and discovered that Nash had been born male.

In most cases, it is impossible to say what motivated these individuals to change their outward appearance. Some, like Mrs. Nash, were no doubt transgender. Others might have done so to live with a same-sex partner as a married couple. When William C. Howard of Canandaigua, New York, died at the age of 50, his widow and two adopted children asked the local undertaker not to prepare the body for burial. They offered to do it themselves. This raised the suspicion of the coroner, who discovered that Howard had been born female. Not that it mattered to her family—as a medical journal later reported, "Howard's ancestral family knew the real condition of things; they do not seem to have looked upon the relationship as at all abnormal."

The First Gay Activists

IF ANYONE was the founder of the modern gay rights movement, it was Karl Heinrich Ulrichs. Born in Germany in 1825, Ulrichs knew he was different from an early age. He later studied to become a lawyer but was fired when his employers learned he was gay.

Albert D. J. Cashier and his gravestone in Saunemin, Illinois.

Portrait courtesy Vicksburg National Military Park

The First Gay President?

WAS JAMES BUCHANAN (1791–1868), America's 15th chief executive, the nation's first gay president? Some historians think so. From 1834 to 1844, while serving as a senator from Pennsylvania, Buchanan lived with William Rufus King (1786–1853) in a Washington, DC, boardinghouse. King was an Alabama senator at the time. The two lifelong bachelors went everywhere together, and Buchanan even began talking with a Southern accent, like King. Former president Andrew Jackson would snicker about the well-groomed pair, calling them "Miss Nancy" and "Aunt Fancy" behind their backs.

James Buchanan (left) and William Rufus King.

Library of Congress (LC-USZC2-2674, LC-USZC2-2488)

The two eventually parted ways when King accepted the job of US Minister to France. After King left, Buchanan wrote to his close friend Cornelia Roosevelt, "I am now 'solitary and alone,' having no companion in the house with me. I have gone a wooing to several gentlemen, but have not succeeded with any one of them. I feel that it is not good for man to be alone, and [I] should not be astonished to find myself married to some old maid who can nurse me when I am sick, provide good dinners for me when I am well, and not expect from me any very ardent or romantic affection."

Buchanan was later elected president, and he was not a very good one. He did little to stop tensions between the North and South in the years leading up to the Civil War and was succeeded by Abraham Lincoln just as the nation split.

Ulrichs then turned to writing. Starting in 1862, he published a series of twelve pamphlets in which he described his own same-sex feelings and speculated on the nature of homosexuality. At first he used a pseudonym—a fake name—calling himself Numa Numantius. Later he switched to his real name, making him the first person to publically "come out"—to voluntarily reveal that he was gay. He didn't use the word *gay*, however, but "urning," a word he made up from Greek literature. Ulrichs called lesbians "urningins."

Ulrichs believed an urning was a "male-bodied person with a female psyche [mind]," and an urningin was a "female-bodied person with a male psyche." Though today this idea seems simplistic and wrong, at the time it was revolutionary. Even more revolutionary was the fact that he talked about homosexuality at all. And he wrote down his thoughts. And *printed* and sent these pamphlets to doctors across Europe!

One of Ulrichs's pamphlets reached Hungarian journalist Károly Mária Kertbeny, who began writing to Ulrichs. In a letter dated May 6, 1868, Kertbeny first used the term "homosexual." Like Ulrichs he had made up the word. It was an odd mix of Greek and Latin terms—*homo* came from Greek, meaning "same," and *sexual* came from Latin. (Kertbeny also invented the word "heterosexual.")

When Kertbeny was a teenager, a gay friend committed suicide because he was being blackmailed. Though Kertbeny was not gay, the tragedy helped him better understand the problems faced by gays and lesbians. Kertbeny later wrote about it in his own series of pamphlets, where he argued for the legalization of homosexuality.

The medical world also started researching homosexuality in the late 1800s, and came up with some strange theories. The idea that gays and lesbians were "inverts," that their minds were somehow wired backward, became a popular theory about homosexuality for the next half century. Doctors also claimed that lesbians preferred the color green. That gay men could not whistle. That lesbians disliked needlework. Imagine—the people who came up with these ridiculous ideas were considered the leading *experts* in the subject.

Around the same time in England, Anglican minister Edward Carpenter read the works of Walt Whitman and decided to leave the church and pursue a life as a writer and lecturer. Carpenter spoke up for the working class, the downtrodden, and social outsiders like gays and lesbians. His writings on homosexuality made a lot more sense than those of the experts, but Carpenter was a gay man, so he knew what he was talking about.

Carpenter's writings were widely read, and he became an early spokesman for gay acceptance in Great Britain in the early 1890s. But soon after, a London scandal changed the public mood and squashed any public acceptance that may have been achieved.

The Trials of Oscar Wilde

THE AUDIENCE rose to its feet, cheering wildly. The opening night curtain had just come down on *The Importance of Being Earnest*, a comedy by Irish poet and playwright Oscar Wilde. Critics loved the play, as they had his earlier theater productions.

But not everyone admired Wilde. Lord John Sholto Douglas, Marquess of Queensberry, was prevented from entering the St. James's Theatre that night. He carried with him a bouquet of rotten vegetables to throw at the

Karl Heinrich Ulrichs, the "Grandfather of the Gay Liberation Movement," 1899. Wikimedia Commons

Where Did the Word "Gay" Come From?

THE WORD "HOMOSEXUAL" IS ONLY ABOUT 150 YEARS OLD, but the word "gay" has been around much longer. It seems to have entered the English language from Old French in the 1100s, where it was *gai*. In English it originally meant "showy," "joyful," or "carefree." But in France during the 1500s it began to be used (as *gaie*) to describe a homosexual person, either male or female. In the United States it was first used widely during World War II, but only within the LGBT community. Not until the 1970s did the general public begin using it.

playwright, if given the opportunity. Douglas had been bullying Wilde for some time. His son, Lord Alfred "Bosie" Douglas, was in a relationship with Wilde, and the Marquess was threatening to cut off his son from his inheritance if the relationship continued.

INVENT A SECRET LANGUAGE

BACK WHEN IT WAS very dangerous to be gay, people had to come up with creative ways to communicate with one another. In London at the time of the Oscar Wilde trial, gay men would sometimes wear a green carnation on their lapel as a signal—*I'm gay*—a code that few non-gay people knew. Later, a red necktie meant the same thing.

A secret language known as Polari started among British theater folk in the 19th century, but it was adopted by the gay community as a way to talk to one another without getting into trouble. Common words and phrases were replaced with uncommon words from sailors' slang, Italian, Yiddish, and other sources. Many words gays and lesbians use today—like camp, butch, and drag—are from Polari.

Think about topics you often talk about with your friends. Now develop a secret language, or at least a small vocabulary of replacement words—your own slang—to speak among yourselves. Make a record of your new terms in a private notebook.

On February 28, 1895, four days after the opening of Wilde's play, John Douglas showed up at the private Albemarle Club and left a crude note accusing Wilde of being gay. Wilde finally decided he'd had enough. He was going to sue his accuser for libel. To libel someone is to make a false statement that damages a person's reputation.

The problem with Wilde's plan was that Douglas was telling the truth. Though Wilde was married and had two sons, he had been having affairs with men. At the 1895 trial, Douglas's lawyer brought several of these men to testify. Douglas was found not guilty of libel, and Wilde was forced to pay Douglas's court costs.

London newspapers then turned on Wilde. One labeled him "the most depraved man in the world." As the scandal unfolded, *The Importance of Being Earnest* was canceled, and Wilde's possessions were auctioned off to pay the bills. And the worst was yet to come. Wilde was charged under the Criminal Law Amendment Act of 1885, which made homosexuality illegal.

"Gentlemen of the jury," the judge at the second trial began, "this case is a most difficult one, and my task very severe. I would rather try the most shocking murder case . . . than be engaged in a case of this description." The government sought to convict Wilde of "gross indecency," but the trial ended when the jury could not reach a verdict.

When a third trial was held, Wilde predicted, "The world is growing more tolerant. One day you will be ashamed of your treatment of me." Yet for the time being, the court was not ashamed at all. Wilde was found guilty. In declaring Wilde's sentence, the judge showed no mercy. "This is the worst case I have ever tried. I shall, under such circumstances, be expected to pass the severest sentence allowed by the law. It is, in my opinion, totally inadequate for such a case as this. The sentence is that you be imprisoned and kept to hard labor for two years."

The gallery gasped and some shouted, "Shame!"

"And I? May I say nothing, my lord?" Wilde asked.

The judge didn't answer, he just waved his hand to the guards, who hustled Wilde out of the courtroom.

Wilde's wife and children changed their names and fled London. When Wilde emerged from prison in 1897, he was a broken man—physically, mentally, and professionally. He moved to France where, on November 30, 1900, he died from complications of an ear injury he suffered in prison. Wilde's body was buried in the Bagneux Cemetery in Paris. He was only 46.

▲ ▼ ▲

Oscar Wilde, circa 1882.
Library of Congress (LC-USZC4-7095)

> "It is funny that men who are supposed to be scientific cannot get themselves to realize the basic principle of physics, that action and reaction are equal and opposite, that when you persecute people you always rouse them to be stronger and stronger."
>
> —Gertrude Stein, in *Wars I Have Seen*, 1945

2

The Birth of a Movement

1900–1930s

August 7, 1915 ▶ Emma Goldman had been lecturing all week at the Turn-verein Hall in Portland, Oregon. She gave a speech on a different topic every night—socialism, war, birth control, and more. Yet her Saturday talk was the most revolutionary: "The Intermediate Sex: A Discussion of Homosexuality." It was the first time anyone had given a lecture on this subject in the United States.

Goldman was not a lesbian; she just hated when the government, big business, or the church used their powers to oppress people. That was clearly the case with homosexuality, as she wrote:

◀ **Gertrude Stein, 1935.** Library of Congress, Carl Van Vechten Collection (LC-USZ62-103680)

Emma Goldman, circa 1911. Library of Congress
(LC-USZ62-48793)

I regard it as a tragedy that people of a differing sexual orientation find themselves proscribed in a world that has so little understanding for homosexuals and that displays such gross indifference of sexual gradations and variations and the great significance they have for living. It is completely foreign to me to wish to regard such people as less valuable, less moral, or incapable of noble sentiments and behavior.

Nobody today has been able to find a copy of her speech from that night, but reports say she did talk about the trial of Oscar Wilde and the writings of Walt Whitman and Edward Carpenter. And after her lecture, a great number of gays and lesbians came to thank her. Goldman later wrote that these people "were often of finer grain than those who had cast them out."

▼ ▲ ▼

Progress

THE 20TH century dawned during the height of what was called the Progressive Era. Social activists, journalists, scientists, and politicians were rethinking every part of daily life. This led to reforms in government, business, and society—regulations for safer food, stronger labor unions, and the right of women to vote.

One of America's greatest reformers was Jane Addams. Born into a wealthy Illinois family, her life's mission changed while traveling through Europe in 1888. There she visited London's Toynbee Hall, the world's first "settlement house." It was founded in 1884 to provide social services and education to the poor workers who lived in East London. Addams returned to Chicago and a year later founded Hull House with her partner, Ellen Gates Starr. The two women had met in college and were a couple for many years.

Hull House was located in the heart of an immigrant neighborhood on the city's near west side. It provided a home for single working women, a gymnasium, a kindergarten, a library, and a community kitchen. It also offered adult education classes and hosted dozens of clubs for children and adults.

Addams believed in an expanded concept of family that she called "combining." These were personal relationships of choice, individuals working together for a common goal.

Hull House was also a hands-on training ground for social workers. One of them, Mary Rozet Smith, would become Addams's partner for the last 40 years of her life. They weren't open about their relationship, but they didn't try to hide it, either. They always slept in the same bed, even while traveling, and in 1904 they bought a home together in Bar Harbor, Maine. Once, during three weeks apart in 1902, Addams wrote Smith, "You must know, dear, how I long for you all the time.... There is reason in the habit of married folk keeping together."

During her life, Addams successfully lobbied the US Congress to outlaw child labor under age 16. This is one of the reasons you're at school today, rather than working in a factory as many kids your age did. Addams was a founding member of the National Association for the Advancement of Colored People (NAACP) and the American Civil Liberties Union (ACLU). In 1931 she received the Nobel Peace Prize, the first American woman to do so. It's not surprising that Addams was once the most admired woman in America.

The Progressive Era also had its moral reformers, the so-called "purity crusaders"—the Union for Concerted Moral Effort, the American Purity Alliance, the National Congress of Mothers, and others. They pushed for crackdowns on any public exhibition of sexuality in books, theater, and art, even related to "traditional" marriage. They often joined forces with temperance crusaders—groups that were hoping to outlaw alcohol.

Though social reformers like Addams greatly improved the lives of America's poor and of women, the purity crusaders would attack and oppress the LGBT community for decades to come.

Magnus Hirschfeld and the Scientific-Humanitarian Committee

BACK IN 1871, a law was added to the books in Germany making male homosexuality a crime. Because of where it appeared in the penal code, it became known as Paragraph 175. Those who opposed it called it "the disgraceful paragraph."

Paragraph 175's biggest enemy was Dr. Magnus Hirschfeld. In May 1897 he founded the Scientific-Humanitarian Committee, the first gay rights organization in Europe ... or anywhere. Its motto was *Per scientiam ad justitiam*: "Through science to justice." The committee had three main goals: repeal Paragraph 175, educate the public about homosexuality, and assist gays and lesbians in their struggle for civil rights.

Hirschfeld started a petition to repeal "the disgraceful paragraph" the same year he started his organization. He sought out famous and little-known people alike. Albert Einstein signed the petition, as did pioneering psychiatrist Sigmund Freud and authors Leo Tolstoy, Thomas Mann, and Herman Hesse, along with more than 6,000 prominent doctors,

Jane Addams, circa 1914. Library of Congress (LC-USZ62-13484)

Dr. Magnus Hirschfeld at a Christmas party, 1917. Magnus Hirschfeld Gesellschaft

scientists, and artists. But the campaign took time; it would be 25 years before Hirschfeld presented the petition to the government on March 18, 1922.

While collecting signatures, the Scientific-Humanitarian Committee started a campaign to educate the public on what it called the "third sex." From 1899 to 1923 the committee published a journal, *Jahrbuch für Sexuelle Zwischenstufen* (the *Yearbook for Intermediate Sexual Types*), the first ever LGBT publication. It contained research papers and stories of interest to the growing gay and lesbian community. The committee mailed the *Yearbook* to every elected official in Germany and wrote thousands of letters to newspapers, churches, judges, police, and anyone else who might help in the cause.

And the efforts paid off! After the turmoil of World War I, Germany saw a relaxation of persecution of gays and lesbians. During the period known as the Weimar Republic, from 1919 to 1933, there were democratic and social reforms. Hirschfeld founded the Institute for Sexual Science in Berlin and, in 1921, the World League for Sexual Reform, which at its peak had 130,000 members. He toured Europe, speaking to overflow crowds in Holland, Austria, Czechoslovakia, and Italy, and later the United States.

The committee even helped produce an "enlightenment movie," *Different from the Others*, to bring its message to the broader public. The silent film showed the fictional story of Paul Körner, a talented violist, who is blackmailed after he is discovered to be gay. Hirschfeld spoke at the 1919 premiere, saying, "The film you are about to see for the first time today will hope to terminate the lack of enlightenment, and soon the day will come when science will win a victory over error, justice a victory over injustice, and human love a victory over human hatred and ignorance."

Henry Gerber and the Society for Human Rights

THE ILLINOIS state clerk who approved the paperwork for the Society for Human Rights (SHR) in December 1924 almost certainly didn't know what the organization was about. SHR's founder and secretary, Henry Gerber, had purposely written the application with vague language. But everyone involved with SHR knew it was a gay rights organization. "Everyone" being the seven people who started it.

Gerber had served for three years in the US Army of Occupation in Germany after World War I, where he witnessed postwar reforms led by Magnus Hirschfeld and others. He wanted the same for the United States, but it was a struggle.

"The first difficulty was in rounding up enough members and contributors so the work could go forward," the often cranky Gerber recalled. "The average homosexual, I found, was ignorant concerning himself. Others were fearful. . . . Some were blasé."

But eventually, in late 1924, Gerber convinced some friends to gather for meetings. There they would discuss ideas to change laws, plan lectures, and build a community. It was mostly just talk, but SHR did publish a newsletter, *Friendship and Freedom*, the first known gay rights journal in the United States. It lasted only two issues.

In July 1925 police raided Gerber's home, seized his typewriter and writings, and threw him in jail. Three other SHR members were also arrested. Though the charges against Gerber were eventually dropped—the police had not gotten a search warrant—he lost his post office job when his bosses found out. Broke and unemployed, he fled to New York and eventually reenlisted in the army.

"We were up against a solid wall of ignorance, hypocrisy, meanness, and corruption," Gerber wrote. "The wall had won."

Gay Paree

"PARIS HAS always seemed to me the only city where you can live and express yourself as you please," claimed writer (and lesbian) Natalie Clifford Barney. And for the early 20th century she was absolutely correct. Following the First World War, Paris became a magnet for authors and artists, many of them gay, lesbian, and bisexual, who would change the modern world.

One lesbian couple, Gertrude Stein and Alice B. Toklas, was at the center of the Paris cultural scene. Stein was a writer, but she is known best for her circle of friends. Every week Stein and Toklas would host a salon—a gathering to talk and exchange ideas—at their apartment at 27 rue de Fleurus. Authors Ernest Hemingway and F. Scott Fitzgerald, singer Josephine Baker, playwright Thornton Wilder, songwriter Cole Porter, and artists Pablo Picasso and Henri Matisse were among those who joined in. Picasso's first Cubist painting was a portrait of Stein.

Toklas acted as Stein's literary agent, and when Stein was eventually talked into writing a memoir of Paris in the 1920s, she wrote it as if Toklas was telling the story. After *The Autobiography of Alice B. Toklas* was published in 1933, the couple toured the United States. They even had tea with Eleanor Roosevelt at the White House. Newspapers widely reported on the pair's 30-year partnership. They were a couple—everyone knew it.

Stein and Toklas lived in the south of France for the final years of Stein's life. When Stein died in 1946, Toklas was by her side. Sadly, Stein's family plundered the couple's art collection

Henry Gerber, and the Chicago home of the Society for Human Rights. Portrait, Wikimedia Commons

Gertrude Stein in her Paris studio, beneath her portrait by Pablo Picasso, 1930.

because Toklas had not been Stein's legal, married spouse. After Toklas died in 1967, she was buried beside Stein in the Père Lachaise Cemetery in Paris, her name etched on the back of Stein's tombstone.

Life Among the Bohemians

IN THE United States, the Progressive Era came to an end after achieving its two main goals: the banning of alcohol ("Prohibition") in 1919 and the establishment of suffrage (voting rights) for women in 1920. Prohibition led to an explosion of "speakeasies"—illegal bars and clubs—where jazz and blues thrived, as did gay culture.

Most cities had neighborhoods where this "Bohemian" life could be found. San Francisco had the Barbary Coast. Boston had Beacon Hill. Chicago, Old Town. New Orleans, the French Quarter. And in New York, Greenwich Village and Harlem were the places to go. In its own strange way, Prohibition forced anyone looking for a drink to act like gays and lesbians had to act—underground, hidden from view, paying off the police to look the other way.

In Harlem, an African American literary and artistic movement called the Harlem Renaissance arose at the same time. Many of its writers, such as Countee Cullen, Langston Hughes, Claude McKay, Angelina Weld Grimké, Alain

Locke, Nella Larsen, Wallace Thurman, Georgia Douglas Johnson, and Richard Bruce Nugent were gay, lesbian, or bisexual. So were sculptor Richmond Barthé and dancer Mabel Hampton.

For the most part, the LGBT writers of the Harlem Renaissance were not publicly open about their sexual orientation. Few people at the time were. But many were open to their friends, and used their writings to carefully discuss LGBT topics. Richard Bruce Nugent's short story "Smoke, Lilies, and Jade" had a gay theme. And Langston Hughes wrote about Harlem's "spectacles of color"—wildly popular drag balls in which men would compete for money and prizes by dressing as women in extravagant gowns. One of the largest of the balls, held at the Savoy Ballroom, could draw audiences of 4,000 people, and the events were usually covered by the city's newspapers.

Gay and lesbian themes began to appear in films and the theater during the 1920s as well. Popular plays such as *The God of Vengeance*, *The Captive*, and *The Children's Hour* had LGBT characters. Though many of these characters were stereotypes—mostly effeminate men and masculine women—it was a step forward to have *any* such characters at the time. Actress Mae West wrote a play called *The Drag* about the gay world, but she was run out of both Connecticut and New Jersey when she tried to stage it. She would have produced it in New York, but the state's 1927 "padlock law" allowed police to close down any theater that had a gay-themed play.

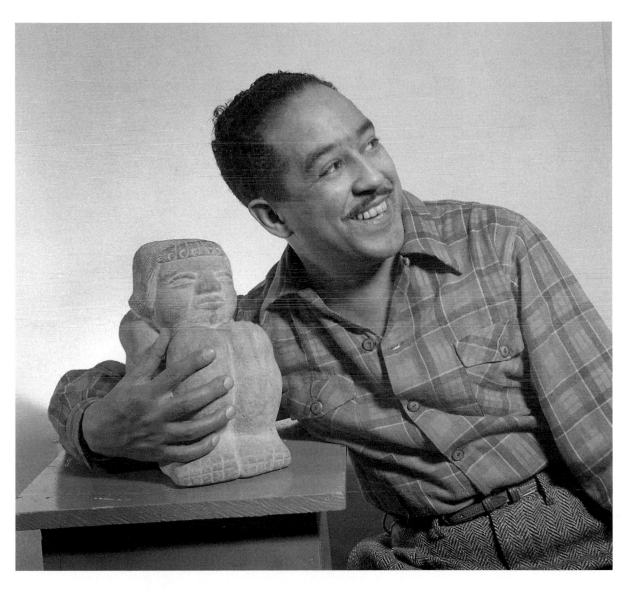

Langston Hughes, one of the greatest writers of the Harlem Renaissance, 1943. Library of Congress (LC-USW3-033841-C)

SINGING THE BLUES

DURING THE EARLY 1900S, music known as the blues, which started in the African American communities in the Deep South, became popular everywhere. A surprising number of early female blues singers were lesbian or bisexual: Bessie Smith, Alberta Hunter, Ethel Waters, and Gertrude "Ma" Rainey, the "Mother of the Blues." One singer in particular, Gladys Bentley, was very open about it. She often performed in a man's white tuxedo, sometimes backed up by a chorus line of male "drag queens," and bragged to her audiences that she had married a woman in Atlantic City.

Many of these performers' most famous recordings are available on YouTube, often with photos, and sometimes with film and television footage. With an adult's permission, go to YouTube and search on the following names and song titles:

Bessie Smith After You've Gone
Alberta Hunter Amtrak Blues
Ethel Waters Am I Blue
Ma Rainey Prove It On Me Blues
Gladys Bentley Worried Blues

Bessie Smith, 1936. Library of Congress (LC-USZ62-88083)

Listen to the lyrics. Can you understand why they are called "the blues"? Whose voice do you like the best? Have you heard any of these songs before?

A Transgender First

BEFORE THE 20th century, people who were transgender had few options. They might feel that they were "born in the wrong body," but they could do little more than change their outward appearance—the clothing and hairstyles they wore. And even that was dangerous. Not until the 1920s did anyone consider surgery to change a person's sex. And then somebody had to be the first to volunteer for what would be experimental medical procedures.

The person who would become Lili Elbe was born in Demark in 1882 and given the name Einar Wegener. Today many believe that Wegener was born intersex—having both male and female sex characteristics. (About one percent of humans show some degree of intersexuality.) Years ago, intersex children were "assigned" a gender by the doctors who delivered them, giving little or no consideration to the child's unique needs.

Wegener was raised as a boy and later married Gerda Gottlieb. Both worked as artists. But one day in the early 1900s, Gottlieb asked her husband to put on women's clothing to substitute for a female fashion model who didn't show up for a drawing session. Wegener then realized that she was more comfortable being female, and she began dressing as a woman more frequently. She also adopted the name Lili Elbe.

The couple eventually settled in Paris. If anyone asked about their relationship, they claimed they were sisters. In time, Elbe met Magnus Hirschfeld, and in 1930 he supervised her first sex-reassignment surgery in Berlin. Not only was it Elbe's first surgery—it was the first of its kind anywhere.

News of Elbe's transition was a hot topic throughout Europe, and even caused the King of Denmark to invalidate Elbe and Gottlieb's marriage. By doing so, the king confirmed that Elbe was now a woman. After all, the reason he objected to their marriage was that two women were now married to one another.

Elbe would go on to have four more surgeries, all performed by Dr. Kurt Warnekros in Dresden, Germany. Sadly, she died from complications from her final procedure. At the time, organ transplants were extremely rare, and antibiotics were unheard of. *Any* kind of surgery was risky.

Lili Elbe's courage to be the first person to undergo sex-reassignment would benefit transsexual people for years to come. However, the years immediately following her death were not good for anyone in the LGBT community.

The Crackdown

AND THEN came the Great Depression. In October 1929, the US stock market crashed and the world economy collapsed. Industries failed and laborers were thrown out of work. People started looking for scapegoats. Had the excesses of the Roaring Twenties led to this financial disaster? The Depression was mainly an economic failure, but some blamed what they saw as the nation's declining morality—the lawless speakeasies and the Hollywood films that glorified crime and sex.

Under pressure from the Catholic Church and other social conservatives, the American movie industry put restrictions on what could and couldn't be shown on screen. The 1930 Motion Picture Production Code banned "immoral" material—passionate kissing, swearing, homosexuality, nudity, and more. It was often called the Hays Code after a man named Will Hays who ran the office that enforced it. The rules were actually written by a Jesuit priest named Daniel Lord. (Not surprisingly, the code also banned showing clergy in a negative way.) Studios had to submit their scripts to a censorship office for approval before they started shooting.

Oddly enough, many of Hollywood's biggest stars at the time were known to be gay, lesbian, or bisexual—actors Tallulah Bankhead, Marlene Dietrich, Greta Garbo, Cary Grant, Katharine Hepburn, Randolph Scott, and Rudolph Valentino, as well as directors like George Cukor and James Whale. Studios added "morals clauses" to their contracts, making it easy to fire anyone if a scandal ever erupted.

However, no studio wanted to fire its biggest stars. To head off rumors, they would feed tabloid magazines fake stories about celebrities dating one another, even if they weren't true. Some gay and lesbian actors were pushed into "lavender marriages" to give fans the illusion that they were heterosexual. Others were threatened; Cary Grant was told he had to end his relationship with Randolph Scott or his contract with Paramount Pictures would not be renewed.

Read All About It

BOOKS ALSO came under fire for "immorality." In 1928, censors in England tried to get the lesbian-themed novel *The Well of Loneliness* banned from publication. It was written by Radclyffe Hall, a British author and lesbian who went by the nickname "John" and often dressed in male clothing.

Those who knew Hall realized the novel was based on Hall's own life. What's more, it wasn't the least bit obscene. But it *was* a plea for tolerance of homosexuality. "You're neither unnatural, nor abominable, nor mad; you're as much a part of what people call nature as anyone else; only you're unexplained as yet," one passage read. "But some day that will come, and meanwhile don't shrink from yourself, but face yourself calmly and bravely. Have courage; do the best you can with your burden. But above all be honorable."

Dangerous stuff!

Apparently some in England thought so. Reviewer James Dudley wrote in the *Sunday Express*, "I would rather give a healthy boy or a healthy girl a [bottle] of prussic acid than this novel. Poison kills the body, but moral poison

A pilot says good-bye to his dying friend in *Wings*—named "most outstanding motion picture production" in the first-ever Academy Awards in 1929. Scenes like this were later forbidden under the Hays Code.

Paramount Pictures/Photofest, © Paramount Pictures

kills the soul." Censors successfully blocked its publication in Great Britain under the Obscene Publications Act, but that only made more people want to read it. Copies were smuggled in from Europe, and later the United States. (People tried to block its publication in America, too, but lost the battle.)

The Well of Loneliness was the most famous lesbian novel at the time, but there were actually hundreds more—more than 500 before 1940—and five times as many about gay men. Most were cheap, poorly written stories, and their characters often met tragedy in the final chapters. Why? According to postal regulations, until the mid-1950s, books with gay and lesbian themes could not be sent through the mail *unless* the subjects came to an unhappy end.

The New Prohibition

IN 1933 the United States ended Prohibition. Almost everyone agreed that trying to ban the sale of alcohol was a failure. Not only did people still drink, but it created new problems, including organized crime, which smuggled the liquor and ran the illegal speakeasies, and corrupt police officers, who took bribes.

In the 1930s, some cities and states had laws against gay and lesbian people gathering or wearing clothes of the opposite gender. As bars reopened, even more cities added these

Marlene Dietrich (1901–1992)

Despite the mostly successful efforts to censor movies of any gay content, some actors and directors challenged the Hays Code in creative ways. The popular Marlene Dietrich dressed in male drag in the films *Morocco* (1930) and *Blonde Venus* (1932). Both times, the plot was written so that she was not a lesbian—technically—but there she was, in a tuxedo, kissing another woman on screen.

Dietrich was born in Germany and began acting and singing in Berlin during the 1920s Weimar Republic. She later moved to Hollywood but was asked to return to her homeland by the Nazi Party after Adolf Hitler came to power. She refused, and applied for US citizenship instead. During World War II she entertained Allied troops and broadcast anti-Nazi messages over the radio to German troops. For this, the bisexual actress was awarded the US Medal of Freedom in 1945. She claimed it was her proudest achievement.

Paramount Pictures/Photofest, © Paramount Pictures

laws. Restaurants and clubs risked having their business licenses revoked as "disorderly establishments" if they dared serve gays or lesbians. Some posted signs: IF YOU ARE GAY, PLEASE STAY AWAY.

Both the Mob and corrupt police used these laws as a way to exploit the LGBT community.

In Greenwich Village, there was even a name for it: "Brown Bag Friday." Crooked police officers would make the rounds of gay clubs on Friday and be handed paper lunch bags filled with cash. And just because a business paid a bribe didn't mean it wouldn't get raided. Often it was the customers that the police were after.

In most US cities, it was illegal for people of the same gender to dance or hold hands. It was also against the law to wear clothing of the opposite gender in public ("masquerading"). In Los Angeles, anyone caught "masquerading" could be punished with a $500 fine and spend six months in prison. Even something as simple as the buttons on a shirt could get a person in trouble—men's shirts usually have the buttons on the right side (with buttonholes on the left), while women's often have the buttons on the left.

To get out of trouble, individuals would do the same thing bar owners did: pay bribes. Activist Hal Call described what it was like in the 1950s: "At that time, $800 [equal to about $7,000 today] bought off the arresting officers and the judge, and it included the attorney's fees, so that one court appearance brought a dismissal."

Gay and lesbian bars fought back the only way they could: by warning their customers. Some would flash their lights when police arrived, and everyone on the dance floor would switch partners to somebody of the opposite sex. The club Gino's in Hollywood would play "The Star-Spangled Banner" on the jukebox. Everyone would stop dancing and split up because, well, *nobody* dances to the national anthem.

The Pink Triangle

As BAD as things were getting in the United States, it was nothing compared to what was happening in Europe, particularly in Germany. The rise of Hitler put an end to all the advances made by Magnus Hirschfeld. In 1921, the doctor had been beaten by a mob of thugs in Munich and left for dead with a fractured skull. He survived, but two years later, Nazi youth threw stink bombs and fired shots into a meeting of supporters in Vienna, injuring many.

Fortunately for him, Hirschfeld was out of the country in January 1933 when Hitler assumed power. In May the Nazis announced they would be purging Germany of books with an "un-German spirit." The Institute for Sexual Science was one of the first attacked. On May 6, as described in *The Brown Book of the Hitler Terror and the Burning of the Reichstag*:

At 9:30 AM some [trucks] drew up in front of the Institute with about 100 students and a brass band . . . then marched into the building with their band playing . . . [T]hey made their way up to the first floor, where they emptied the ink bottles over manuscripts and carpets and then made for the bookcases. They took away whatever they thought was not completely unobjectionable . . . taking down to the [trucks] basket after basket of valuable books and manuscripts. . . .

A few days later, all the books and photographs, together with a large number of other works, were publically burned on Opera Square. . . . A bust of Hirschfeld was carried in a torchlight procession and thrown onto the fire.

Hirschfeld fled to a small apartment in Nice, France. There he wrote in his journal, "I have resigned myself to the idea that I shall never see Germany, my homeland, again." He died on May 14, 1935, his 67th birthday, four years before the start of World War II.

The Nazis began rounding up gay men in 1934. A year later, Paragraph 175 was amended to make same-sex kissing, hugging, and even *thoughts* illegal. As many as 50,000 men were imprisoned. Some, but not all, were later sent to concentration camps, where their uniforms were marked with an upside down pink triangle—the *Rosa Winkel*.

Lesbians were also imprisoned, though not as many. They were marked with black triangles as "anti-social," their primary "crime" being their unwillingness to bear children for the Third Reich, defying the Nazi slogan, *Kinder, Küche, Kirche*—Children, Kitchen, Church.

Fewer than 4,000 gay and lesbian prisoners survived the Holocaust. As the camps were liberated, many still faced arrest—Paragraph 175 was still in place—and their imprisonment was kept on their police records. (East Germany didn't do away with the law until 1988, and West Germany not until 1994, at reunification.) For decades, many histories of the Holocaust did not include the persecution of those who wore the pink and black triangles.

▲ ▼ ▲

"Ask anyone who served in World War II, in any branch of the service, and they will tell you they knew someone who was gay then and it didn't bother them."

—Dan Murphy, US veteran

3

In the Shadows

1940s–1950s

June 1944 ▶ The Battle of Saipan was a brutal, bloody fight that raged for 25 days. More than 3,400 US soldiers died in the fight for the small South Pacific island. One casualty was the boyfriend of Jim Warren. The two men were in the same army unit and had talked about starting a life together after the war.

Warren's boyfriend was shot by Japanese forces while trying to take out one of their machine-gun nests. Medics brought him back to a tent, bleeding from several bullet wounds, and Warren was able to say his last good-byes.

"I stood there and he looked up at me and I looked down at him, and he said, 'Well Jim, we didn't make it, did we?' And tears were just rolling down my cheeks," Warren remembered. "There were maybe seven or eight people standing there, and I was touching his hand and we were talking. Somebody later said, 'You were

◀ **Troops aboard the USS *John Ericsson* arriving in New York, August 1945.**

Library of Congress (LC-DIG-ppmsca-19287)

pretty good friends,' because I had been openly crying. . . . I said, 'Yes, we were quite good friends.'"

▼ ▲ ▼

World War II

MORE THAN any other event, World War II launched the modern gay rights movement in the United States. During the conflict, 16 million men and 350,000 women served in the US armed forces. For most troops, it was their first time away from their hometowns. This gave gay and lesbian soldiers opportunities to meet others like themselves and the freedom to confront the feelings they shared.

Just before the war, the American Psychological Association advised the US military to "test" recruits for homosexuality. However, the War Department needed troops, gay or not. Recruits were simply asked, *Do you like girls?*, to which most men, gay or straight, could honestly answer yes. (Women were not similarly screened.) Fewer than 5,000 gay men were barred from service during the five-year war.

"[I] knew an awful lot of gay people but nobody, with one exception, ever considered not serving," remembered Chuck Rowland, who was in the army. "We were not about to be deprived of the privilege of serving our country in a time of great national emergency by virtue of some stupid regulation about being gay." Some, who knew about Hitler's persecution of gays, enlisted specifically *because* they were gay.

Back in the States, two million women entered the industrial workforce, building aircraft, ships, bombs, and jeeps. And because it was dangerous to have long hair in a factory, nobody much cared if a woman had short hair or wore slacks, both of which could have sparked harassment in the 1930s. Lesbian bars flourished in ports and manufacturing cities.

And after the war ended, gay and lesbian veterans returned to the United States with a new perspective. Many ended their service in cities like San Francisco, New York, Los Angeles, and San Diego and decided to stay to set up new lives. Sadly, some had no choice.

No Thank You for Your Service

AS WORLD War II came to an end, first in Europe and then in the Pacific, fewer troops were needed, and the Pentagon began discharging more and more gay service men and women. Despite their service, some were court-martialed. Many others were denied honorable discharges and were thrown out with Section 8 or "undesirable" discharges (often called blue discharges because they were printed on blue

Alan Turing (1912–1954)

Few people have influenced modern life as much as Alan Turing. A brilliant mathematician, Turing led the British team that cracked the Enigma code. The German high command used Enigma to send messages to its navy during World War II. The code-breakers, working in a secret facility at Bletchley Park in the English countryside, used a machine called a "Bombe" to decipher Enigma messages. The Bombe was about six and a half feet tall and seven feet long, and it weighed about a ton. It was designed by Turing and was an early version of the modern computer.

Being able to decipher the enemy's communications gave the Allied forces a great advantage, and some say it shortened the war by two years. Turing was awarded the Order of the British Empire in 1946, the highest honor in the United Kingdom, though it was kept secret for years, as was everything that happened at Bletchley Park.

After the war, Turing continued to lay the groundwork for modern computer science. But in 1952 he was investigated and put on trial for being gay. Convicted under the same law as Oscar Wilde, he was fired from his government position as a security risk... *the guy who helped win the war*. To keep out of prison, Turing agreed to undergo female hormone therapy, sometimes called chemical castration, which doctors thought would "cure" his homosexuality.

His career in ruins, Turing grew depressed, and on June 8, 1954, he committed suicide by eating a poisoned apple. No public apology

Codebreaker Hut 8, where Alan Turing's team broke the Enigma code.

Portrait, © National Portrait Gallery, London

was made until 2009, when British Prime Minister Gordon Brown issued this statement: "On behalf of the British government, and all those who live freely thanks to Alan's work, I am very proud to say: We're sorry, you deserved so much better." On December 24, 2013, Queen Elizabeth signed a full pardon.

paper). Roughly 5,000 soldiers and 4,000 sailors were given blue discharges during and just after the war.

While not the same as dishonorable discharges, blue discharges were just as bad. They made the veterans ineligible for benefits under

**Edythe Eyde/Lisa Ben,
1987.** Photo by Robert Giard,
courtesy Estate of Robert Giard

the GI Bill—unemployment support, disability benefits, and home, business, and college loans. Veterans who received blue discharges could not be treated at VA hospitals, even for injuries suffered in combat, and they were stripped of any service medals they had received. And worst of all, many employers would not hire anyone who had received one.

Forced out of the closet by the military's policies, yet having pride in their service to the country, a number of gays and lesbians in New York formed the Veterans Benevolent Association (VBA) in 1945. It was mostly a social organization but also supported members as they looked for work or fought for their rights or benefits. The VBA had about 100 members, though its popular dances would attract as many as 500 guests.

Many gay and lesbian veterans started their own businesses after the war, often because they couldn't find work elsewhere. Others did so because they wanted to live as they chose without the fear of being fired for being gay.

Vice Versa

IN JUNE 1947, Edythe Eyde was working as a secretary at RKO Pictures in Hollywood. Her boss was a minor executive who always wanted her to look busy even if she had nothing to do,

mostly because it made *him* look busy. *Type something*, he suggested. *Don't sit and read a book.*

Eyde had been thinking of writing about her life in Los Angeles. Two years earlier she had moved to the city and met a new group of friends at her apartment. When they learned she was gay, like they were, they took Eyde to a women's softball game. She was bored, but she liked meeting new people.

But then they took her to the If Club, a lesbian bar. "When we all walked in there, . . . someone was bringing a birthday cake to one of the booths. There were some girls sitting there, and they were singing 'Happy Birthday.' I looked around me, and tears came to my eyes . . . and I thought, *How wonderful that all these girls can be together.*" Eyde felt right at home.

And so Eyde started writing *Vice Versa*, "America's Gayest Magazine." She didn't realize it, but *Vice Versa* was also America's *only* gay magazine. Each issue was just a few pages long. Eyde would put eight sheets of paper into her typewriter, separated by carbon paper, so her typing would show up on each of the eight pages. Then she would type each page with carbon paper again, making sixteen copies altogether. She handed the copies out to her friends and told them to pass the copies to somebody else once they'd finished.

To avoid trouble, Edythe Eyde didn't use her real name in the magazine, but wrote under the pen name Lisa Ben. (Get it?) *Vice Versa* was an upbeat mixture of book and movie reviews, poetry, news, letters, and essays. Sometimes she wrote about her vision of the future, as she did in the September 1947 issue. The essay, "Here to Stay," imagined a different world: "I venture to predict that there will be a time in the future when gay folk will be accepted as part of regular society."

Vice Versa only lasted nine issues, from June 1947 to February 1948. Eyde left RKO for another job and wasn't able to continue writing it. Plus, as she later admitted, "I wanted to live it rather than write about it."

Bestselling Breakthroughs

IN THE years following the war, two books were published that changed the way Americans thought about homosexuality. One was a dry, 804-page study full of graphs and tables, and the other was a collection of essays from somebody that nobody had ever heard of. Surprisingly, both were runaway bestsellers—everyone was talking about them.

Sexual Behavior in the Human Male by Alfred Kinsey was published in January 1948. Most just called it the Kinsey Report. Over several years Kinsey, a zoologist at Indiana University, and his research team had interviewed 5,300 men about the most personal details of their private lives. What he found shocked American society: he claimed that 37 percent of male adults reported having had at least one same-sex experience, and that 10 percent of men were mostly or exclusively gay. One in ten!

In 1953 Kinsey issued *Sexual Behavior in the Human Female* based on interviews with 5,940 women. The Kinsey Reports showed that there were far more gays, lesbians, and bisexuals than anyone suspected. This gave tremendous hope to those living in the closet—pretty much the entire LGBT community in the 1950s.

Many didn't want to believe Kinsey's findings or claimed his study was flawed. But the American Statistical Association reviewed his work and declared it "a monumental endeavor" and scientifically sound.

The other bestseller, *The Homosexual in America* by Donald Webster Cory, was published in 1951. Cory was the pen name of Edward Sagarin, a Brooklyn man who had read the Kinsey Report and felt there needed to be a book written by an actual gay man, not a scientist studying gay men.

In addition to its honest description of what it was like to be gay in America, the book attacked the hypocrisy and cruelty of

Alfred Kinsey, 1953. Photofest

MAKE UP A SONG PARODY

AFTER SHE QUIT WRITING *Vice Versa*, Edythe Eyde (still as Lisa Ben) had a career writing song parodies about lesbian and gay life. She would take popular songs and change the lyrics—"The Girl That I Marry" and "Frankie and Johnnie"—and perform them at lesbian and gay shows.

You can write your own song parody. What topic do you find interesting? Life at school? Something funny or interesting that happened to you or your family? Choose a simple song that you already know, something easy like "Yankee Doodle Dandy," that you think might fit your subject. Find the original lyrics online and print them out, then write your own words to replace the originals. When you are satisfied with what you've written, find an instrumental version of the original song on YouTube and use it to accompany you as you sing your new version.

mainstream society. "Tolerance is the ugliest word in our language," Sagarin wrote. "I can't see why anyone should be struggling to be tolerated. If people are not good, they should not be tolerated, and if they are good, they should be *accepted*."

Sagarin also suggested a pathway to gay liberation: come out of the closet and demand to be treated like everyone else. "[If an appeal were made] to the American traditions of fair play and equality of opportunity, I am personally convinced that American minds will change."

That would happen eventually, but not just yet.

The Lavender Scare

DESPITE THE work of Kinsey, Sagarin, and others, the 1950s were some of the darkest years for LGBT citizens in the United States. With the Cold War came fear that sinister elements threatened the fabric of American society—radicals, Communists, and "sex perverts," the term then used for gays and lesbians.

People today are familiar with the Red Scare, the effort to remove "Communist sympathizers" from government and entertainment. But few know of the Lavender Scare that happened at the same time. The purge of gays and lesbians from federal jobs began quietly in the late 1940s. The effort gained new momentum in 1950 when Senator Joseph McCarthy began attacking "Communists and queers."

The Senate Subcommittee on Investigations took up the hunt. Despite being unable to find a single case of a gay or lesbian employee being blackmailed, the senators recommended that action be taken. "Homosexuals and other sex perverts are not proper persons to be employed in government for two reasons," the subcommittee reported. "First, they are generally unsuitable, and second, they constitute security risks." Senator Clyde Hoey then added: "Government officials have the responsibility of keeping this type of corrosive influence out of the agencies under their control. One homosexual can pollute a government office."

Federal agencies began searching for gay and lesbian employees. Investigators followed every rumor and accusation, and if there was even a hint of homosexuality, the employee was fired or forced to resign. During the 1952 presidential election, Dwight Eisenhower used the campaign slogan "Let's Clean House," and soon had his chance. On April 27, 1953, shortly after taking office, Eisenhower signed Executive Order 10450. Under the order, federal employees could be dismissed for "any criminal, infamous, dishonest, immoral, or notoriously disgraceful conduct, habitual use of intoxicants to excess, drug addiction, or sexual perversion."

If this wasn't bad enough, at the same time almost every state in the union prohibited gays and lesbians from holding licensed professional jobs, including doctors, lawyers, teachers, stockbrokers, undertakers, and beauticians. The Eisenhower administration even put pressure on private companies, international agencies (like the United Nations), and foreign governments to follow its lead. A similar anti-gay purge swept England at the same time.

Most Americans supported the government-led witch hunts. Rev. Billy Graham, the nation's most prominent religious leader, praised the effort for "exposing the pinks, the lavenders, and the reds who have sought refuge beneath the wings of the American eagle."

Before it was over, 5,000 gays and lesbians had been forced from their government jobs, more than 1,000 from the State Department alone. During the early 1950s, the number of gays and lesbians who were fired was twice the number of suspected communists who lost their jobs. To those being persecuted, it must have felt as if their government had abandoned them. Did the US Constitution not apply to them as well?

A few brave activists would soon test that question, starting with freedoms guaranteed them under the Bill of Rights, including the rights to free speech, a free press, and peaceable assembly.

The Mattachine Society

ON NOVEMBER 11, 1950, Harry Hay invited some of his friends—Bob Hull, Dale Jennings, Chuck Rowland, and Rudi Gernreich—to his Los Angeles home. They had all talked before about starting an organization for gay men. Now Hay wanted to make it happen.

At first they called themselves the Society of Fools, but they later renamed themselves the Mattachine Society. (The Mattachines were medieval court jesters who were allowed to speak openly to the monarchy.) They also said the organization was "homophile," meaning "same love," which they thought was more accurate than "homosexual."

In the beginning the meetings were just a chance to get together and talk. Members would discuss the Kinsey Report, their dreams of starting a shelter for runaway kids, or more practical matters, like legal advice.

Then in February 1952, one of the society's members, Dale Jennings, was arrested by a police officer with the L.A. vice squad. Jennings had been entrapped, and he asked Mattachine to help him fight back in court. What made the Jennings case unique was that Dale Jennings admitted to being gay and was willing to challenge the police.

"Think of all the guys that have gone through this completely alone," Jennings thought to himself. "I must stand up for myself, and for them."

At trial, the arresting officer was caught in a lie, and the case collapsed. When the jury couldn't agree on a verdict, the judge dropped the charges. Newspaper reports brought national attention to the society. Mattachine soon had many more members and chapters as far away as Chicago.

But with success came problems. Some new members thought the group's founders were too radical. It all blew up at the group's first "constitutional convention" held in April 1953 at the First Universalist Church in Los Angeles.

The 1951 Mattachine Christmas party. Members (l to r): Harry Hay (top), Konrad Stevens (lower left), Dale Jennings, Rudi Gernreich, Stan Witt, Bob Hull, Chuck Rowland, and Paul Harvey. J. Gruber Papers, Gay & Lesbian Center, San Francisco Public Library

About 150 delegates gathered for what was the first *open* gathering of gay men in the United States. It soon became clear that many wanted to unseat Harry Hay and his loudmouthed, troublemaking friends. Some were angry that Hay had sent a questionnaire on gay rights to candidates running for L.A. City Council. Was he trying to get them in trouble?

Within six months, all the founders were gone. The Mattachine Society became an organization looking for social acceptance at any cost. "We do not advocate a homosexual culture or community, and we believe that none exists," the new president said. Statements like that weren't a smart way to build a gay organization. The group slowly died.

ONE, Inc.

EVEN BEFORE the Mattachine Society fell apart, some of its members were looking for something different. "I'm tired of talking," Johnny Button said at one gathering. "I want to do something! Why don't we start a magazine?" Other Mattachines, like Jim Kepner, had been thinking the same thing, and in 1952 they launched ONE, Incorporated. They got the name from a line in an essay by Thomas Carlyle: "A mystic bond of brotherhood makes all men one."

Unlike Mattachine, which had very few women, ONE welcomed everyone. The organization published the first issue of *ONE* magazine in January 1953. The price? Twenty-five cents. Its editor, Martin Block, described the magazine: "We weren't going to go out and say you should be gay, but we said, 'You can be proud of being gay.' You could look yourself in the mirror and say, 'I'm me, and isn't that nice?'... That in itself was radical."

And this radical idea *did* help many. A reader in 1957 wrote, "I have been miserable these past few months because I had no one to discuss my problems with. But now that I have found your magazine I feel much better about my whole situation."

But not everyone appreciated *ONE*. When the October 1954 issue came out, the Los Angeles post office seized it. *ONE* was "obscene, lewd, lascivious, and filthy," and therefore couldn't be sent through the mail. In reality, the issue had nothing "obscene" in it, just an article by a lawyer saying that freedom of the press in the United States wasn't entirely free, particularly for gays and lesbians. Now the post office was proving the lawyer's point.

ONE decided to sue. It lost at the first trial, and twice more when it appealed to higher courts. But the magazine didn't back down. In its November 1955 issue, writer David L. Freeman stated that gays were everywhere, including "key positions with... the FBI (it's true!)." On FBI Director J. Edgar Hoover's orders, two

agents went to ONE's offices to demand that the author "put up or shut up." They met with its editor, William Lambert.

Because *ONE* had so few people working on it, most of its staff used multiple pen names, all fakes. It made the magazine appear less like the rinky-dink operation it was. "David L. Freeman" was one of the many pen names of Chuck Rowland, but the FBI didn't know that. Neither did they know that the editor sitting in front of them, "William Lambert," was really a man named Dorr Legg.

"Lambert" told the agents he'd cleared the article with a lawyer (which was true) and that he stood behind "Freeman's" work. The FBI didn't care. The discussion went around in circles, and eventually the frustrated agents left. Legg watched the pair go, thinking, *They're not so smart.*

For five months the FBI tried to dig up information on Freeman and Lambert. By the time the agents figured out that Freeman was actually one of Chuck Rowland's pen names, Rowland had left the magazine. So what could they do? They recommended to Hoover that "no further action be taken."

Meanwhile, *ONE*'s censorship case finally reached the US Supreme Court. The justices didn't even bother with oral arguments. On January 13, 1958, they unanimously agreed that *ONE* had every right to be sent through

ACTIVITY
FORM A CLUB

HAVE YOU EVER WANTED to start a club with your friends? Maybe you have the same hobby, play the same sport, or are fans of the same singer or artist.

First, you need to come up with a name for your club. Do you want it to sound clever? Mysterious? Or clear and straightforward?

Next, decide how the club will be run. Will you elect a president or captain? Will you all vote on what you choose to do each time you get together? Whatever you decide, everyone should play a part.

Do you think you need to keep a record of your activities, either through a blog, a journal, or photos you take? This could be a good way to find new members—show them how much fun you're having!

If you want to get fancy, there are other ideas for your club in this book—you can create a club logo (page 77), or a club button (page 53), or make a flag (page 91).

the mail. It was the first positive ruling on an LGBT issue from the nation's highest court.

Don Slater wrote in *ONE*'s next issue, "By winning this decision *ONE*... has made not only history but law as well and has changed the future for all US homosexuals. Never before have homosexuals claimed their right as citizens." It also did wonders for subscriptions. Not only did thousands of LGBT people hear about the magazine for the first time, they also knew it could be mailed to them without any trouble.

Dr. Evelyn Hooker

BACK IN 1945, just after the war, a man named Sam From invited psychologist Dr. Evelyn Hooker and her husband to visit him in San Francisco for Thanksgiving. One evening From took the Hookers to Finocchio's, a nightclub that featured female impersonators, and they had a wonderful time. After the show, From confessed that he had brought Dr. Hooker for another reason. "We have let you see us as we are," he announced, "and now it is your scientific duty to make a study of people like us." At the time most psychologists treated LGBT people as if they were mentally ill, and From knew this wasn't true. He and his friends were just fine—happy, healthy, and responsible. He wanted Hooker to prove it.

Dr. Hooker was surprised, and at first she said no. She couldn't study *him*—they were friends, she pointed out. "He replied that they could get me a hundred men, any number that I wanted. Sammy would not let me go." The idea definitely intrigued Hooker. How would she do a study? And what would she find?

By 1953, Dr. Hooker came up with an idea. She selected 30 average gay men and 30 average heterosexual men and gave them three common psychological tests. She then showed other psychologists the men's responses, but did not tell the doctors who was straight and who was gay. At the time, most doctors believed it would be simple to pick out the gay subjects based only on their answers.

And what did Hooker discover? This group of smart, respected psychologists couldn't identify the gay subjects based only on their "psychological adjustment" as measured by the tests. And in fact, overall they judged the anonymous gay subjects to be slightly higher "functioning" than their straight counterparts.

What was going on? Hooker believed there was a simple explanation: up until this point, most of what psychologists knew about homosexuality came from patients who had come to them for help, either to "cure" themselves or as the result of a court order. By and large, they were an unhappy and troubled group of patients. And of course, the doctors had their own ideas

CONDUCT AN INKBLOT TEST

ONE OF THE THREE psychological tests Evelyn Hooker gave to her subjects was the Rorschach Test, also known as the Inkblot Test. In it, subjects are shown ten cards with different splotchy images and asked to describe what they see. According to Rorschach, their answers give clues as to the way their subjects think.

You'll Need

► 5 sheets construction paper
► 1 jar dark tempera paint
► Pen
► 1 sheet notebook paper

To see how differently people think, LGBT or not, you can conduct your own Inkblot Test on your family and friends. First, you need to make a set of inkblots. Holding the paper with the long sides on top and bottom, fold each sheet down the middle, top to bottom. When you're done folding, open each sheet back up and dribble a *small* amount of tempera paint on one side of the fold.

Fold the other half over and gently press down to squish the paint inside. This will create "bilateral symmetry"—a mirror image around the center fold line (all Rorschach ink-

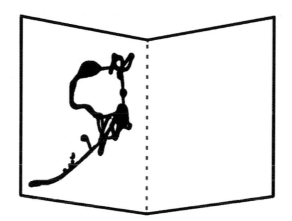
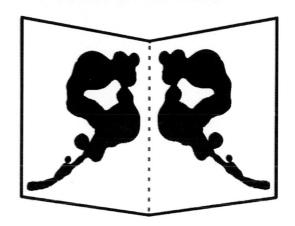

blots look like this). Then open the paper back up and set it aside to dry. Continue with the rest of the sheets.

Once the paint is dry, number the inkblots 1 through 5 with the pen. Now you're ready. Show each inkblot to a variety of people and ask them to describe what they see. Record their answers on the notebook paper. Once you've tested several people, compare their answers. Did everyone see the same thing?

Card I in the Rorschach Test. Wikimedia Commons

about homosexuality, often based on nothing more than hunches and stereotypes. Now Hooker had scientific evidence that gays and lesbians were pretty much like everyone else.

Hooker's pioneering research would eventually lead the psychiatric community to change its thinking. Yet sadly, the man who convinced Dr. Hooker to do the work never saw its results. Sam From died in a car crash before Dr. Hooker's study was published.

Transgender Superstar

CHRISTINE JORGENSEN was resting from her third operation in a Copenhagen hospital when a stranger entered her room holding a telegram. It was the headline from the December 1, 1952, edition of the *New York Daily News*: BRONX GI BECOMES A WOMAN. DEAR MOM AND DAD, SON WROTE, I HAVE NOW BECOME YOUR DAUGHTER.

How could my parents have done such a thing? Jorgensen thought. They had been so supportive when she told them she was going to Denmark for sex-reassignment surgery, a still almost unheard-of procedure. (At the time it was essentially illegal in the United States.) Now her personal letter to them was splashed across the front page of her hometown paper!

The hospital was soon flooded with telegrams, phone calls, and unannounced visitors. A reporter from New York called and demanded she speak. "All of America is anxiously awaiting a statement from you!" he bellowed. But Jorgensen only wanted to hear from her parents.

A letter arrived several days later. Her mother wrote how the *Daily News* reporter had learned of Jorgensen's operation and wanted them to comment, and said that if they didn't, he'd run the story anyway. The letter went on,

After a long talk, we all decided that it would be the best way of presenting the truth, . . . [rather] than to make matters worse by allowing them to slant everything badly. . . .

I do hope you can be as calm as possible. We are all big enough to face facts with strength and courage, as you have already shown. Do take care. We are okay, so don't worry. . . .

Love, Mom

Christine's father added his own note at the bottom:

Keep your chin up, everything will be all right. We are with you all the way.

Love, Dad

After remaining mostly silent while she finished her recovery in Denmark, Jorgensen returned to New York in February 1953. As she stepped off the airplane she was greeted by more than 300 reporters and photographers. "I thought for a moment that I had entered Dante's Inferno, as flash-bulbs exploded from all directions and newsreel cameras whirred," she recalled.

Jorgensen hadn't been looking for publicity. After her surgery, the 26-year-old American planned to return to the States and her career as a photographer, but her newfound celebrity changed all that. Everyone wanted to know more about her. "If I sneezed, it was duly reported as an event," she joked. And that was almost true—a pack of reporters even followed her to the Motor Vehicle Bureau when she renewed her driver's license.

Given the public's general attitude toward gays and lesbians at the time, it was encouraging to see that the nation's first famous transgender woman was treated so well. Yes, there were some who criticized and condemned her, but mostly Jorgensen was treated with respect. She appeared on television and radio shows, and was a guest of honor at many charity fundraisers.

Jorgensen eventually developed a nightclub act—a little singing, a little dancing, and a few tame jokes. She also returned to photography, and eventually the media firestorm died down. Through it all, her willingness to be the public

face for the emerging transgender community did much to raise the public's understanding of the issue.

The Daughters of Bilitis

PHYLLIS LYON and Del Martin, a San Francisco couple, got a call from Rose Bamberger in September 1955. "Would you like to be a part of the group of six of us who are putting together a secret society of lesbians?"

"We said, 'YES!!' because we would immediately know five more lesbians than we did, which was . . . AMAZING," remembered Lyon.

Originally it was just supposed to be a social club. "[Bamberger] wanted it to be in people's homes and she wanted it to be so we'd be able to dance . . . so that we wouldn't get caught up in police raids and we wouldn't be stared at by tourists," Lyon said. "You couldn't dance in the bars in those days. And she loved to dance."

Four couples—Rose and Rosemary, Mary and Noni, June and Marcia, and Phyllis and Del—officially launched the Daughters of Bilitis (pronounced "bill-EE-tus") with a party on October 19, 1955. The group's unusual name was drawn from Pierre Louÿs's collection of poetry, *Les Chansons de Bilitis* (*Songs of Bilitis*), which had a lesbian theme. If anyone got suspicious and asked what they were up to, they could claim they were a poetry club. The

Christine Jorgensen, 1953.
Everett Collection, Inc./Alamy

Lavender Scare was still going on—they had to be careful. So before they danced, they would close the curtains.

The Daughters of Bilitis (DoB) was the first organization for lesbians in the United States. It was open to any woman 21 or older who was a "gay girl of good moral character." The club's colors were sapphire and gold, and its motto was "Qui vive"—"On the alert." And though it started as a social club, the group got into politics soon enough. Several of the founders who

The Daughters of Bilitis at a Sausalito gathering. Del Martin is at the far left, Phyllis Lyon at the far right. Courtesy Gay, Lesbian, Bisexual, Transgender Historical Society, Lyon Martin Papers

were more interested in dancing, bowling, and horseback riding later left the group.

On the whole, though, more people were joining than quitting, including a young woman from Philadelphia named Barbara Gittings. She had been searching for a lesbian community for some time, and eventually learned about DoB. Gittings booked her next vacation to California.

"I called up when I arrived in San Francisco and they invited me to a meeting which was being held the following night, and that next night I was in a room with twelve other lesbians for the first time in my life and, oh, what a thrill that was!" she recalled. "It was a business meeting where they were planning the publication of their magazine, *The Ladder*. I just sat there and reveled in their company. These were nice women."

The Ladder

THE FIRST issue of *The Ladder* came out in October 1956. It was twelve pages long. The Daughters of Bilitis printed 175 copies and sold them all. The magazine's name was meant to suggest an escape from "the well of loneliness" that Radclyffe Hall had described years earlier.

In the beginning, *The Ladder* wasn't political; it just had book reviews, news reports, poetry, research reports, and letters. And for the first few years it struggled to survive. "The movement was entirely run by people who had no money to give.... I remember days like the day the box of pens came, the day the box of brown envelopes came," Barbara Grier recalled. "These were big moments in the life of a publication like *The Ladder*."

Still, readers loved it. "L.L." from California wrote, "Thank you a thousand times over for your publication!... I can't begin to tell you how lonely it is walking alone.... I have an intense longing to communicate with other persons like myself, who live on the outside."

In September 1958, Barbara Gittings started a DoB chapter in New York. By 1960, there were five chapters—San Francisco, New York, Chicago, Rhode Island, and Los Angeles—with a total of 110 members. Yet for every paying member, there were many more who followed the DoB's activities. And not just other lesbians.

Just before the DoB's first four-day conference began on May 27, 1960, San Francisco police showed up at the Hotel Whitcomb. Del Martin was ready—she smiled and invited them to come in and look around. Inside they found 200 women and a few men, all gathered to hear presentations on the theme, "A Look at the Lesbian." After the police determined that everyone was dressed in "proper" attire, they left.

LEARN "THE MADISON" LINE DANCE

FOR YEARS same-sex couples could be arrested for dancing together in public. One way around this was line dancing, sometimes called "no touch" or social dancing—dozens, and even hundreds of people performing the same dance steps at the same time, usually facing the same direction. One of the most popular was "The Madison," which started in Columbus, Ohio, but became internationally popular, and not just in the LGBT community.

You can learn the basic steps to the Madison by watching an instructional video on YouTube—search on "Madison Line Dance Demo." (It also appears in the movie *Hairspray*.) Once you've mastered the basic steps, try a few of the special steps—the Double Cross, the Cleveland Box, and the Two Up and Two Back. Get your friends and family to learn the Madison, too—the more people you can get to line dance at the same time, the more fun you'll have.

This harassment would continue. "You never knew what was going to happen. This was particularly true of some of the first gay conferences," Gittings remembered. "How were hotel people going to treat you? Were they going to give you a hassle? Was there going to be a disruption from outside? Would police arrive and trump up some kind of stupid charge against us? All those things happened on occasion."

Pushed Too Far

ON DECEMBER 20, 1957, astronomer Frank Kameny was fired from his job with the US Army Map Service. Kameny's boss had learned that he was gay and expected him to slink away in shame. Boy was he wrong. The firing transformed Kameny from a mild-mannered scientist into one of the greatest heroes of the LGBT civil rights movement.

"I decided that my dismissal amounted to a declaration of war against me," the World War II veteran recalled. He hired a lawyer to get his job back. They went to US District Court and lost. They went to the US Court of Appeals and lost again. All this time, Kameny was still out of a job—*any* job. "For about eight months in 1959 I was living on twenty cents' worth of food a day.... A big day was when I could afford twenty-five cents and put a pat of margarine on my frankfurters and potatoes."

Believing the case was hopeless, the lawyer quit. Kameny was left to write his own petition to the US Supreme Court, which he did in January 1961. He laid out his case, writing:

As an employer, the government's only proper concern is with the employee's work and conduct during working hours. It is not for the government-as-employer to intercede in the employee's private affairs.... Our government exists to protect and assist all of its citizens, not, as in the case of homosexuals, to harm, to victimize, and to destroy them.

By March he received his answer: the case was denied. Years later he recalled what he thought when he got the bad news: "I am right and they are wrong and if they won't change I will have to make them." He might have lost this battle, but the war wasn't over.

The Black Cat

AS THEY had every Sunday evening for several years, the staff at the Black Cat pushed four tables together in the crowded club to form a makeshift stage. Cocktail waiter José Sarria then climbed onto the stage as the customers cheered. Sarria wore red, high-heeled shoes and the dress of a Spanish gypsy, a purple orchid pinned at his shoulder. Nearby, James McGinnis (whom everyone called "Hazel") began playing the piano, and the crowd hushed as Sarria launched into a song from the opera *Carmen*.

Sarria had entertained Black Cat audiences with his one-person opera parodies since 1958. Each performance was different; he would change the lyrics to comment on the news or tease a person in the crowd. But the performances always ended the same way: Sarria would ask everyone to stand, grab the hands of the people closest to them, and join in singing his version of "God Save the Queen."

> *God save us nelly queens*
> *God save us nelly queens*
> *God save us queens.*
> *From every mountainside,*
> *Long may we live or die,*
> *God save us nelly queens*
> *God save us queens!*

"I sang the song as a kind of anthem, to get them realizing that we had to work together, that we were responsible for our lives. We could change the world if we weren't always hiding," he later explained. *"God save us nelly queens*, that's what you are, be proud of it and get off your butt and do something about it. It was a silly song, but serious too."

Sarria didn't go unnoticed by authorities. How could he? His Sunday opera was one of the most popular shows in San Francisco. Undercover police officers were often in the audience during the sing-a-long. Sometimes Sarria would lead the crowd out of the bar and down to the local police precinct where they would all serenade those who had been arrested during bar raids.

LGBT Hero: Lorraine Hansberry (1930–1965)

One of the most famous contributors to *The Ladder* was playwright Lorraine Hansberry. She wrote under the initials LHN (for Lorraine Hansberry Nemiroff). She also wrote for *ONE* magazine and was one of the first members in the New York City chapter of the Daughters of Bilitis.

Hansberry is best known for writing *A Raisin in the Sun*, a play about a black family's attempt to move into a restricted white neighborhood. It was the first play by an African American woman to open on Broadway, and was named Best Play by the New York Drama Critics Circle Award in 1959.

Hansberry often included realistic gay and lesbian characters in her plays. Sadly, she wrote very few; Hansberry died of pancreatic cancer at age 34.

A *Playbill* for Hansberry's best-known play, *A Raisin in the Sun.* Photofest

PLAYBILL
ROYALE THEATRE

A RAISIN IN THE SUN
by Lorraine Hansberry

WWW.PLAYBILL.COM

None of this amused the police or politicians. The state once tried to shut down the Black Cat, but owner Sol Stoumen sued and won. Police tried a different tactic one Halloween, but Sarria outsmarted them. At the time, a law forbade men from wearing women's clothing "with the intent to deceive," yet people could dress up on

Halloween. Just after midnight, the cops burst into the Black Cat to arrest any cross-dressing men still there. They found plenty, but Sarria had pinned felt buttons to each of their outfits that read, "I am a boy." Since there was no intent to deceive, nobody was breaking the law.

"The police knew a potential lawsuit when they saw one," said Sarria. "That was the beginning of the end of the Halloween raids."

José Sarria at a regular Sunday performance at the Black Cat, early 1960s. Courtesy ONE National Gay & Lesbian Archives, Hal Call Papers

Rumblings of a Movement

AS THE 1950s came to an end, life in the United States began to be more open. Some credit the poets and writers of the Beat Generation—Allen Ginsberg, Jack Kerouac, Peter Orlovsky, Gregory Corso, and others. They had met each other in New York during the 1940s, but they didn't gain much national attention until the late 1950s.

Allen Ginsberg became front-page news with his book-length free verse poem *Howl* in October 1956. The poem spoke of subjects rarely discussed at the time, including Ginsberg's own homosexuality. It was published by Lawrence Ferlinghetti, owner of City Lights Bookstore in San Francisco. When store manager Shigeyoshi Murao sold a copy of *Howl* to two plainclothes police officers, he was arrested. So was Ferlinghetti. Both were charged with obscenity.

The trial of Ferlinghetti and Murao was followed by newspaper and magazine readers coast to coast. Famous writers, poets, and critics testified about the poem's importance, and the judge eventually ruled it was not obscene. Ginsberg (and the rest of the Beats) could not have asked for better publicity.

Though many of the Beats were gay or bisexual, they didn't work much with the growing homophile movement. To the Beats, the

Mattachine Society and the Daughters of Bilitis probably looked just as square as everyone else. Still, the LGBT movement learned a lot from watching the Beats, including the idea that maybe they didn't have to ask anyone's permission to live the life they wanted to live.

"When are American homosexuals going to stop sitting around pitying themselves, excusing themselves, hiding their faces and bemoaning their lot?" an editorial in the March 1959 issue of *ONE* asked its readers. "When are they going to roll up their sleeves and do some of the hard work and the fighting that any segment of society must do to defend its own rights?"

Or, as Allen Ginsberg said, "For those of us who were homosexual it was suddenly the realization, 'Why are we being intimidated by a bunch of jerks who don't know anything about life? Who are they to tell us what we feel and how we're supposed to behave? . . . Why not sort of dish it back and start talking openly?'"

And that's just what they did.

Peter Orlovsky (left), Gregory Corso (center), and Allen Ginsberg (right) in the 1959 film *Pull My Daisy.* Phototest

Signs carried by protestors read: "HOMOSEXUAL PREFEREN[CE] IS IRRELEVANT [T]O ANY Employme[nt]", "HOMOSEXUAL AMERICAN CITIZENS— OUR LAST OPPRESSED NATIONAL MINORITY"

"I decided then that I had run long enough. All of us have to make our own compromises in life. I decided not to hide any more."

—Frank Kameny

4

Out of the Closets

1960s

December 2, 1964 ▶ Randy Wicker and a few of his friends showed up early for the lecture at the Cooper Union Forum. Dr. Paul Dince, an associate professor at New York Medical College, was scheduled to lecture on "Homosexuality: A Disease."

Wicker's group carried signs saying WE REQUEST 10 MINUTES OF REBUTTAL TIME and passed out flyers to everyone who had come to hear the talk. At the end of the lecture, Dince invited Wicker to respond.

The activist made the most of his time. Wicker pointed out where psychiatric studies contradicted each other, and how the studies were often conducted on unhappy or unwilling subjects. And who said anyone needed to be "cured"? Finally, he explained how psychiatrists themselves stood to profit from these harmful,

◀ **Frank Kameny at the first Annual Reminder outside Independence Hall, July 4, 1965.**

Photo by Kay Tobin. © Manuscripts and Archives Division, The New York Public Library

unproven methods aimed at "curing" gay patients.

"Applause for the challenger topped applause for the lecturer, who appeared stunned for a moment by the reaction of the audience," *The Ladder* reported.

▼ ▲ ▼

A League of One

RANDY WICKER, whose real name was Charles Gervin Hayden Jr., lied to get into the New York Mattachine Society in 1958—you were supposed to be 21 or older to join, and he was only 20. But Wicker desperately wanted to do something to help the LGBT community. *Anything.* And he wasn't the type who waited for permission.

"He was, let's say, a disturbing acquisition for the movement," Mattachine's president, Arthur Maule, later admitted. Once, without asking, Wicker passed out leaflets announcing a Mattachine meeting and 300 people showed up—far more than could ever fit in the group's second-floor office. The angry landlord kicked the organization out.

In early 1962, frustrated by Mattachine's take-it-slow approach, Wicker formed his own group: the Homosexual League of New York. Wicker was president, vice president, treasurer,

secretary . . . and the only member. But he had an organization and a fancy title, which was all reporters and radio hosts apparently cared about. That year he was interviewed on WBAI-FM radio in New York, which soon led to interviews that appeared in *Newsweek*, *Harper's*, the *Washington Post*, the *New York Post*, and the *New York Times*. Friends often joked that he was the "Gay Crusader" and asked him where his cape was.

Wicker also organized the first known gay rights demonstration in the United States. In 1962, Wicker and his friend Craig Rodwell picketed the New York City draft board at the Whitehall Induction Center. They were demanding that the Department of Defense stop releasing information on rejected gay draftees to employers. Nothing much came of it.

Wicker returned to protest again on September 19, 1964. This time, ten people marched.

José Sarria Runs for Office

THROUGHOUT THE 1950s, José Sarria would routinely go before the San Francisco Board of Supervisors—basically the city council—to complain about police harassing the LGBT community. In 1961, he got the crazy idea to run for a seat on the board.

"I went down to City Hall and found out what I had to do to run for office. I had to have twenty-five signatures and twenty-five dollars," Sarria said. There were five open seats on the board but only nine people (including Sarria) who were gathering signatures. With so few running, his chances to win were good!

Sarria turned in his petition just 12 hours before the filing deadline, and when the politicians saw it they panicked. They immediately rushed to get others on the ballot. Before the end of the day, there were 34 people in the race. "But that didn't stop me. I still campaigned," Sarria said.

My platform when I ran was "Equality Before the Law." The San Francisco Court House had just been built and that was the slogan [engraved] on it and I said, "This is what my slogan will be. . . . I saw that there were two interpretations of the laws and that they were trying to make gay people second-rate citizens. I've never been a second-rate citizen.

"I campaigned in schools and before organizations of all kinds. I went on radio. . . . I spoke Spanish, so I was capturing the Spanish vote," he recalled. On Election Day, he came in ninth with 5,613 votes. Not bad. But not a victory, either.

Sarria's campaign was part of a growing political movement in San Francisco. In 1962

MAKE A BUTTON

TO FINANCE HIS POLITICAL WORK (and put food on the table), Randy Wicker ran a button-making business during the 1960s. By the end of the decade, he was the biggest supplier of political buttons on the East Coast, which he sold through a store called Underground Uplift Unlimited. He created buttons with Frank Kameny's "Gay Is Good" slogan (see page 58), and for many other movements and causes.

You'll Need
► 1 piece of blank paper
► Pencil
► 1 old button
► 1 blank self-adhesive address label (large enough to cover button)
► Scissors

You can make your own design out of an old button and a blank address label. Decide what you want to put on it: a slogan, a logo, or maybe a picture. First, use a pencil to sketch your design onto blank paper. Second, trace around the button onto the blank address label. (If the label is too small, use two labels placed side by side.) Copy your design onto the label, use scissors to cut it out, and then affix it to the old button.

several gay and gay-friendly San Francisco establishments formed the Tavern Guild. Its goals were to fight police harassment and corruption, and to register LGBT voters. Each time there was a raid, they signed up more voters.

The Tavern Guild split up a year later, but in September 1964 its remnants became a more powerful organization: the Society for Individual Rights (SIR). They didn't just register voters. For the first time they asked politicians to meet with them, and they would pass out campaign material for the candidates they liked. The first was Diane Feinstein, who years later would become a US senator.

To show that they were concerned with the larger community, SIR raised money for local causes—for youth, the elderly, the deaf, and others. And in April 1966, SIR opened San Francisco's first gay community center. Unlike the Tavern Guild, SIR lasted a long time—17 years.

Going After Uncle Sam

AFTER THE Supreme Court refused to hear his case, Frank Kameny decided he needed to start organizing and finding people like himself to fight the government's antigay policies. Along with friend Jack Nichols, he launched the Mat-

City & County of SAN FRANCISCO City Election, Tuesday, Nov. 7th *1961*

Elect

JOSÉ JULIO SARRIA

Supervisor

"Equality!"

Flyer from José Sarria's 1961 campaign. Courtesy Gay, Lesbian, Bisexual, Transgender Historical Society, José Sarria Papers

Sarria's New Group

IN 1965, JOSÉ SARRIA WAS AT A LOW POINT. "I lost the election, my mother died, the [Black] Cat closed. What else could happen to a person?" he wondered. But rather than sit back and feel sorry for himself, he founded a charitable organization known as the International Court System, also called the Imperial Court System, or ICS. Members compete in elaborate drag balls to raise money for worthy causes—AIDS charities, breast cancer, homeless shelters, guide dogs for the blind, domestic violence programs, food banks, college scholarships, and disaster relief. Sarria crowned himself the "empress" of the first San Francisco chapter. Del Martin and Phyllis Lyon helped found the ICS and were given the title of "Duchesses."

The ICS is currently the largest LGBT charitable organization in the world, with 70 chapters in the United States, Canada, and Mexico. Several chapters have raised more than a million dollars since they began.

tachine Society of Washington (MSW) on November 15, 1961. The group had nothing to do with the original Mattachine Society, other than its name.

Because it was located in Washington, DC, and because Frank Kameny was running the show, MSW decided it would focus its energy on the federal government—the job dismissals, the military's treatment of gay and lesbian servicemembers, or any other unfair treatment of the LGBT community. And it wouldn't be shy.

In 1962, the 40-member group announced its plans by sending a press release to the president, the vice president, every member of the cabinet, every senator, every representative, every Supreme Court justice, and everyone else in power in the capital. Representative John Dowdy of Texas was so furious he entered MSW's material into the *Congressional Record*, giving the organization unexpected but welcome publicity.

But it was FBI Director J. Edgar Hoover who was angriest of all. Frank Kameny put Hoover on the mailing list for *The Gazette*, the society's newsletter. Kameny had heard whispers around Washington, the same whispers heard earlier by the writers at *ONE*: Hoover was gay. (Based on what we know today, this rumor was likely true.)

One day Kameny got called down to FBI headquarters by agent John O'Beirne. At the meeting, O'Beirne demanded to know why Hoover was being sent *The Gazette*. Kameny said he thought Hoover would be interested in MSW since it was a civil rights organization and the FBI investigated other civil rights matters.

Agent O'Beirne was not amused. "Mr. Hoover would like to be taken off your mailing list," he demanded. Kameny said he'd bring it up with other members of the Mattachine board, but no promises. Later, back at the office, Kameny thought about everything O'Beirne had said in the meeting and realized that the agent knew too much about MSW—more than the organization had ever included in its newsletters and press releases. In other words, the group was being spied upon.

So Kameny responded to O'Beirne with his own demands: remove and destroy all of the files the FBI was collecting on them, have Hoover send a letter saying it had been done, and only then would they consider taking the director off its mailing list. *Maybe.*

Few people ever called the FBI's bluff. Agent O'Beirne sent a memo to Hoover recommending that they cease communications with MSW, and Kameny never heard from them again. Kameny was so pleased he wrote a brochure that was widely distributed to LGBT groups, government employees, and military servicemembers: "How to Handle a Federal Investigation."

FBI Director J. Edgar Hoover was not a fan of the homophile movement. Author's collection

It was a numbered list that reminded readers of their constitutional rights. Item 9 reflected his new attitude:

9. Insist that you be treated with the full respect and dignity due ALL American citizens in every status, by ALL their public servants, at ALL levels, at ALL times. If you are not so treated, walk out and do not return until you have received, in writing, an apology for past improper treatment, and assurances of future proper behavior.

California Hall

ON JANUARY 1, 1965, San Francisco's California Hall was lit up like a Hollywood movie premiere. Elegantly dressed couples walked in past the bright spotlights. Some smiled and some posed for the cameras, though many were secretly terrified. The photographers weren't with the press, they were from the San Francisco Police Department, the same people who had brought in the lights. And the paddy wagons. And the riot gear. The cops wanted this New Year's Day Mardi Gras Ball—a fundraiser for the Council on Religion and the Homosexual (CRH)—shut down. Immediately.

Inside the hall, Phyllis Lyon and Del Martin worked the front table, checking tickets and welcoming guests. Every fifteen minutes or so the police barged through doing "fire and health inspections," they said. For many of those attending, a good number of whom were local ministers and their wives, it was an eye opener. Did gays and lesbians have to put up with this harassment all the time?

After several of these "inspections" the lawyers for CRH decided to block the officers. "That's enough!" Herb Donaldson and Evander Smith said. "If you want to come in,

Council on Religion and the Homosexual

THE VERY FIRST US ORGANIZATION TO HAVE THE WORD "HOMOSEXUAL" as part of its name also had the word "religion." San Francisco's Council on Religion and the Homosexual (CRH) was formed in May 1964 by the Daughters of Bilitis, the Mattachine Society, and Glide Memorial United Methodist Church. That spring, five lesbians, ten gay men, and fifteen liberal clergy met for three days in nearby Marin County. For most, it was the first time to talk at length, honestly, about the differences between their communities. The Glide pastors led a largely African American congregation and had been involved in the struggle for civil rights, so what they heard sounded sadly familiar. After the conference, the pastors were taken to local bars to show how the gay community had been forced to hide in the shadows.

In addition to the California Hall fundraiser, in 1965 CRH organized the first Candidates' Night for those running for office in the Bay Area, to learn their positions on LGBT issues. CRH no longer exists, but Glide Memorial United Methodist Church still serves the San Francisco area, working to alleviate suffering and break the cycles of poverty and marginalization.

you're going to have to get a search warrant." The police just arrested the two lawyers instead. (Four other people were also arrested that night.)

Donaldson and Smith were taken to the station, booked, and released on bail before the party ended. When they got back to California Hall they witnessed police officers with movie cameras marching across the dance floor, filming everyone. Around 11 PM, police declared the fundraiser over and pushed everyone to the exits.

The next morning CRH called a press conference at Glide Memorial United Methodist Church. All dressed in their Sunday best, seven ministers blasted the actions of the police department. In time they would launch Citizen Alert, a 24-hour phone hotline to report police misconduct.

When the lawyers' case went to trial, the police department testified first. The judge wasn't impressed. "It's useless to waste everybody's time following this through to its finale," he announced, then ordered the jury to declare the CRH lawyers not guilty. They didn't even get a chance to present a defense. The case was dismissed!

The events at California Hall were reported in newspapers across the United States. Soon gays and lesbians everywhere were thinking, *Hey, maybe I should move to San Francisco.*

The Annual Reminder

ON THE East Coast, the LGBT community was getting bolder as well. Frank Kameny formed an alliance with Barbara Gittings of the New York Daughters of Bilitis in 1963, and in autumn 1964 hosted a gathering in Washington, DC, of the East Coast Homophile Organizations—ECHO. The group voted to picket the White House. Kameny insisted they have a dress code: men in business suits and ties, women in modest dresses and heels. He also announced the group's intentions in an article in the March 1965 issue of *The Ladder*:

> *It is time that we begin to move from endless talk . . . to firm, vigorous action. We are right: those who oppose us are factually and morally wrong. . . . We must demand our rights, boldly, not beg cringingly for mere privileges, and not be satisfied with crumbs tossed to us.*

On Saturday April 17, the day before Easter, ten ECHO members—seven men and three women—showed up outside the north fence

Ernestine Eckstein (front left) of the New York Daughters of Bilitis at the Third White House Picket, October 23, 1965. Photo by Kay Tobin.
© Manuscripts and Archives Division, The New York Public Library

of the White House. They did not publicize the details of their plan for fear that they'd be turned away before they even started... but that also meant that no media were there, either. They marched in a circle for two hours, carrying signs.

HALT GOVERNMENT'S WAR AGAINST HOMOSEXUALS

FIFTEEN MILLION US HOMOSEXUALS PROTEST FEDERAL TREATMENT

US CLAIMS NO SECOND-CLASS CITIZENS— WHAT ABOUT HOMOSEXUAL CITIZENS?

"We had no idea what police would do or how they would behave... nothing happened, nobody threw rocks at us. It was magnificently successful," Kameny said.

ECHO was just getting started. The next day, 29 people marched outside the United Nations in New York to protest dictator Fidel Castro's persecution of gay Cubans. In the weeks to follow, they picketed the State Department and Civil Service Commission in Washington, the Pentagon, the White House (again), and on July 4, Independence Hall in Philadelphia, where 39 people marched.

The protest outside the birthplace of American independence became a regular event, starting in 1965. ECHO named the July 4 event the Annual Reminder. "It was thrilling," Gittings remembered. "You knew you were doing something momentous. People would stare at you. They had never seen self-declared homosexuals parading with signs."

"Gay Is Good"

IN JULY 1968 FRANK KAMENY CAME UP WITH A CATCHPHRASE for the early LGBT civil rights movement: "Gay Is Good." He got the idea from "Black Is Beautiful," a popular slogan in the African American community during the 1960s. "If I had to specify the one thing in my life of which I am most proud," Kameny later said, "it would be that."

Kameny's slogan reflected the movement's new attitude. "It is time to open the closet door and let in the fresh air and the sunshine; it is time to hold up your heads and look

the world squarely in the eye as the homosexuals that you are, confident of your equality," he wrote. "It is time to live your homosexuality fully, socially, psychologically, emotionally, and in every other way. *Gay is good*. It is."

Frank Kameny (center, holding sign), 1970. Photo by Kay Tobin. © Manuscripts and Archives Division, The New York Public Library

Others, like Martha Shelley, were not as thrilled. "I did not like parading around while all these vacationers were standing there eating ice cream and looking at us like we were critters in a zoo," she said.

Yet one of those vacationers made a comment to Kay Lahusen, Gittings's partner, who reported it in *The Ladder*. It took "a lot of guts to stand up for your rights," the person said.

Indeed it had.

The First Riots

NOT EVERYONE in the LGBT community was as committed to nonviolence as the people at California Hall or the picketers at the Annual Reminder. Many, particularly transgender individuals and teenage runaways, had long been victims of police harassment and brutality. It was only a matter of time before they started to fight back.

The first documented LGBT riot took place in May 1959—nobody quite remembers the exact day—at Cooper's Donuts in downtown Los Angeles. One evening officers with the Los Angeles Police Department (LAPD) showed up at the late-night coffee shop and started asking people to show their IDs. When they ordered two customers into their squad car, people started throwing donuts. Cups of coffee followed, and the police fled to their cruiser and

LGBT Hero — Bayard Rustin (1912–1987)

In the long struggle for civil rights in the United States, few people have matched the dedication and accomplishments of Bayard Rustin. Born into a Pennsylvania Quaker family, Rustin began a life of activism in the 1930s. He was a pacifist and a labor organizer, and in the early days of the 1955–56 Montgomery Bus Boycott, he trained Martin Luther King Jr. in nonviolent tactics.

Rustin was also gay. Because of this, Congressman Adam Clayton Powell Jr. forced King to remove Rustin from his post at the Southern Christian Leadership Conference in 1960. But three years later, civil rights leader A. Philip Randolph demanded that Rustin be asked to organize the 1963 March on Washington for Jobs and Freedom (the event where King delivered his famous "I Have a Dream" speech). Just days before the event, the racist Senator Strom Thurmond denounced Rustin as gay on the Senate floor. This time, King stood by Rustin under intense pressure from the media and some civil rights leaders. The march went on as planned.

As a gay civil rights leader, Rustin was not alone. Grant Gallup, a white civil rights worker, recalled, "Many of us who went south to work with Dr. King in the '60s were gay. I remember a plane going down from Chicago—there were six priests and three of us were gay. A lot of gay people who could not come out for their own liberation could invest their same energies in the liberation of black people."

Bayard Rustin (left) organized the 1963 March on Washington. Library of Congress (LC-USZ62-133369)

called for backup. Reinforcements soon arrived, and several rioters were arrested.

On April 25, 1965, Philadelphia police were called to Dewey's Deli over a disturbance. The manager had threatened to deny service to anyone who was wearing "nonconformist clothing," and about 150 protesters showed up for a sit-in. Police arrested three teenagers and a lawyer who was assisting them. They were all found guilty of disorderly conduct. Dewey's was picketed again, and there was another sit-in. Eventually the deli backed down and promised "an immediate cessation of all indiscriminate denials of service." The protesters won!

A year later, in San Francisco, a two-day riot erupted at Compton's Cafeteria. Members of the city's transgender community often gathered at the all-night establishment, managed by an older gay gentleman who liked the crowd. But after he died, relations between Compton's and its customers had become strained, and police would often walk through and harass the customers.

Then one night in August 1966 the police were called because of an unruly customer. When officers tried to arrest her she doused them with hot coffee. The cops fled, and the restaurant erupted into a free-for-all. Angry customers overturned tables and smashed the front windows with sugar shakers. When another squad car arrived, the mob trashed the cruiser and set a corner newsstand on fire.

In the wake of the Compton Cafeteria Riot, the San Francisco Police Department established its first community relations liaison officer to work with the transgender community, Sergeant Elliott Blackstone. With somebody finally paying attention to the community's concerns, including the issuing of ID cards to help transgender citizens find work, anti-LGBT violence in the city's Tenderloin district fell.

Another uprising took place a few months later in Los Angeles. On January 1, 1967, just moments after midnight, patrons at the Black Cat Tavern (not connected to the San Francisco bar) were giving each other New Year's Day kisses. Plainclothes officers from the LAPD told the kissers they were under arrest. When the patrons asked to see the policemen's badges, the cops clubbed them with their guns and one officer said, "That's all the identification you need." People fled to the New Faces bar across the street, chased by the police. By the end of the night, 16 had been arrested.

Angry citizens immediately formed the group Personal Rights in Defense and Education—PRIDE—to protest police harassment. On February 11, about 500 people picketed on the sidewalk outside the bar and passed out flyers to motorists and pedestrians. A police commander ordered the crowd *not* to use the word

The Metropolitan Community Church

THE **LAPD's** RAID ON THE **PATCH** unexpectedly launched what has become the largest LGBT church in the world. Troy Perry was at the bar that night with a date, Tony Valdez, who was arrested. Valdez later claimed that God didn't care about the suffering of gay people. Perry, a Pentecostal preacher who had been run out of his Florida church when the congregation learned he was gay, vowed to prove him wrong.

On October 6, 1968, Perry held the first service of what would become the Metropolitan Community Church (MCC) in the living room at his rented Los Angeles home. He used his coffee table as the altar. Twelve people attended. Nine of them were friends who came to give Perry emotional support if it failed.

Perry made social justice a major part of MCC's ministry. Much of the early LGBT activism in Los Angeles was the work of Perry and church members. Protests, parades, telephone hotlines—MCC was always there. Perry and his church also organized the first LGBT lobby In Washington, DC.

On June 12, 1970, Perry officiated the marriage of Neva Joy Heckman and Judith Ann Belew, the first of its kind in the United States. Nothing prevented a congregation like MCC from blessing a gay or lesbian union (though it was not a legally binding marriage), and so they did—150 times over the next four years.

MCC grew, and in October 1970 the church purchased its first building in Los Angeles. That building was destroyed by arson the night of January 26–27, 1973. Unbroken, more than 1,000 people showed up the following Sunday for an outdoor service in the street across from the rubble.

Arsonists have targeted MCC churches 21 times, and far worse, have killed four clergy. But the ministry continues. Today, MCC has more than 170 churches in 37 different countries.

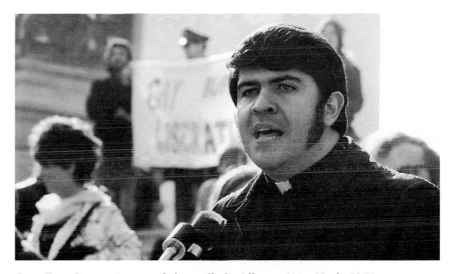

Rev. Troy Perry at a gay rights rally in Albany, New York, 1971.
Photo by Diana Davies. Manuscripts and Archives Division, The New York Public Library

"homosexual" in their chants, which of course made them shout it even louder.

On August 17, 1968, the LAPD went into the Patch, a gay bar, and began to arrest some of

its customers. For holding hands. For dancing. The bar's owner, Lee Glaze, hopped on stage and grabbed a microphone. "It's not against the law to be a homosexual, and it's

Activist Martha Shelley at the Oscar Wilde Memorial Bookshop, 1969.

Photo by Diana Davies. Manuscripts and Archives Division, The New York Public Library

not a crime to be in a gay bar!" he shouted, and said he'd pay the bail of anyone arrested. Unlike during so many raids before, the customers stayed put (or kept dancing) and the *police* fled. Glaze then chased the officers back to the Harbor Division Station with 25 customers, but not before stopping at a florist shop to buy bouquets for their arrested friends.

Here We Are

ON MARCH 7, 1967, 40 million Americans got an up-close look at gay life when CBS television aired a documentary, *The Homosexuals*. And though it did break new ground—by discussing the topic at all—it was filled with stereotypes, errors, and outright hostility. Frank Kameny, the most active, well-spoken gay spokesperson on the East Coast, appeared onscreen for just 16 seconds, although a sightseer who happened to walk by ECHO's White House protest during filming, spoke three times as long. "I think these people are a fit subject for a mental health program," the man offered, but admitted, "I'm qualifying all of this that I'm a poor country boy from West Virginia and this is amazing to me."

The LGBT community was treated far better by Phil Donahue, a daytime talk show host out of Dayton, Ohio. Donahue had his first openly gay guest in 1968, and viewers could call in and ask questions. Some were friendly and supportive, others were cruel and judgmental, but most were just curious. Donahue's show eventually went nationwide, and for decades it was a safe outlet to discuss LGBT issues on television.

Gays and lesbians had a lot to learn about themselves too. That's why Craig Rodwell opened America's first LGBT bookstore in New York's Greenwich Village on Thanksgiving weekend in 1967. The Oscar Wilde Memorial Bookshop became a meeting place for the city's gay residents before there was a community center. Rodwell was the only employee for the first year and a half. The store had a large plate glass window in front, a window that was often smashed by vandals.

The Stonewall Uprising

SOME SAY it was the heat, others the full moon. But the real reason customers at the Stonewall Inn in New York City battled with the police on June 28, 1969, was simple: they were fed up. The New York Police Department's (NYPD) Sixth Precinct had raided five other gay bars in the preceding three weeks, and the Stonewall had been raided just three days earlier. And now the police were back.

Around 1:20 AM, Deputy Inspector Seymour Pine and seven officers entered the popular Greenwich Village bar, blocked the front door,

Maurice Sendak (1928–2012)
LGBT Hero

One of the greatest gay writers of the 1960s was children's author Maurice Sendak. At the age of twelve he saw the Disney movie *Fantasia* and decided he would be an artist. Though he had begun illustrating books in the 1950s, it was the publication of *Where the Wild Things Are* (which he also wrote) in 1963 that made him famous. The book received the Caldecott Medal for the Most Distinguished Picture Book of the Year. It was the only time he ever won the award, but he was a runner up seven more times, more than any other children's writer/illustrator. Sometimes criticized by those who believed his books are too dark or scary for children, Sendak was unapologetic. "I refuse to lie to children," he said.

Where the Wild Things Are.
Photofest

and turned on the overhead lights. (Four more undercover cops were already inside.) The Stonewall's managers and bartenders were arrested for selling liquor without a license and taken outside to a paddy wagon. The cops then demanded all 200 customers show their IDs. One by one they were allowed to leave, but not men who were dressed in drag or women in men's clothes.

The customers mostly did as they were told, but others gave the officers flak. As they

BUILD A TELEIDOSCOPE

AFTER BEING DRIVEN OUT of the Mattachines, the society that he had founded, Harry Hay temporarily retreated from the spotlight. In 1962 he met John Burnside III, a scientist specializing in optics, and they became a couple. Together they invented and patented a "Telescopic Kaleidoscope," which they later called a Teleidoscope, and they opened a factory in New Mexico to build them.

You'll Need

► 1 sheet of paper
► Pencil with eraser
► Ruler
► 3 thin plastic mirrors
► Scissors
► Lens (clear glass ball, magnifying glass, or clear drinking glass)

You can build a simple Teleidoscope using three plastic mirrors, a cardboard toilet paper tube, tape, and a clear glass ball.

First, trace the end of the tube onto a sheet of paper. Then draw a triangle within the circle, as shown. Make all three sides of the triangle the same size (you might want to use a pencil with an eraser, because it may take you a couple of times). Measure one side of this triangle—this is your mirror width. Now

measure the length of the tube—this is your mirror length.

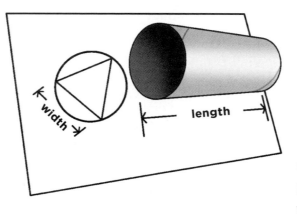

Cut three thin plastic mirrors—you can find them at a dollar store—to the width and length measured. They should be much longer than they are wide. Tape them together in a triangular tube with the reflective sides facing inward. Then slide the attached mirrors into the cardboard tube.

Finally, you need a lens. You can use a clear glass ball, magnifying glass, or a clear drinking glass filled with water. (Look through the side without tipping the glass.) Hold the lens in front of the tube while looking through from the other end.

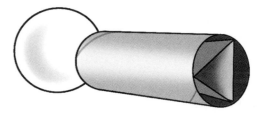

Look around the room through your Teleidoscope. What do you see? Once you've proven that it works, share your Teleidoscope with your family and friends.

emerged, some took bows for the crowd gathering in Christopher Park, just across the street. A few even cracked jokes: "Have you seen Maxine? Where *is* my wife—I told her not to go far!" said one man as he exited.

"Instead of the homosexuals slinking off, they remained there, and their friends came," Pine remembered, estimating that the crowd had grown tenfold since last he looked. People had been phoning their friends. The crossdressers were loaded into the paddy wagon, but when the police turned away, they jumped out and disappeared into the crowd.

Rey "Sylvia" Rivera, a transgender teen, recalled: "Everybody's looking at each other. 'Why do we have to keep putting up with this?'"

Onlookers began throwing pennies. "Here's your payoffs!" they shouted at the cops, taunting them. The Stonewall Inn, like many gay bars at the time, was Mafia owned—"Fat Tony" Lauria ran the place and paid off corrupt police to look the other way.

Finally, the last person was taken from the bar, a "butch" lesbian who the police roughed up while trying to shove her into a squad car. Two times she escaped from the backseat, but the officers grabbed her and tossed her back in. The third time, while kicking at the officers, she yelled to the crowd, "Why don't you guys do something?!"

"Flip the paddy wagon!" people screamed. Coins turned to bottles, and bottles turned to paving stones and bricks. Somebody slashed the tires on the police car that still held the woman.

"I'll never forget the looks on the cops' faces," bystander A. Damien Martin later said. "They looked like someone who had just been bitten by a trusted pet, a look of astonishment and fear at the same time."

The paddy wagon raced off with three squad cars—one riding on four flat tires. The ten cops left behind fled into the bar and used tables to barricade the front door. Rioters yanked a parking meter out of the sidewalk and used it as a battering ram on the entrance. Somebody set a trash can on fire and tried to throw it through the front window, but it was protected by plywood on the inside. Police found a fire hose inside the bar and blasted water out through holes at their attackers. "I had been in combat situations [but] there was never any time that I felt more scared," Pine admitted.

Forty-five tense minutes later, two fire trucks pulled up, followed by police reinforcements wearing riot helmets and swinging billy clubs. And though the officers in the Stonewall Inn were rescued, the battle raged through the early morning. The NYPD's Tactical Police Force chased rioters down the nearby alleys and streets, but caught very few. Amid the

chaos and tear gas, a group of drag queens in heels formed a Broadway-style kick line and broke into song:

> *We are the Village girls!*
> *We wear our hair in curls!*
> *We wear our dungarees,*
> *Above our nelly knees!*

Word of the early morning uprising drew 2,000 people to the Village the next night, where the gutted Stonewall served free soft drinks to happy, liberated patrons standing in the broken glass. About 400 police arrived later, and another clash erupted. The cops weren't any more successful in stopping the uprising than they had been the night before. And while most of the police were surrounding the Stonewall Inn, a group of street youth snuck over to the quiet precinct station and plastered pink-and-blue EQUALITY FOR HOMOSEXUALS bumper stickers on all the squad cars and patrol wagons.

Just by chance, Martha Shelley of the Daughters of Bilitis was leading a group of Boston women on a tour of Greenwich Village establishments that night. When they came upon the battle, one of the visitors turned to Shelley and anxiously asked, "What's going on here?" Shelley responded, "Oh, it's a riot. These things happen in New York all the time."

Another clash erupted on Sunday, the third night. Remarkably, only seventeen people were arrested that entire weekend, and seven of them were Stonewall employees who had been taken away in the first paddy wagon. Martin Boyce, who had witnessed it all, first thought, *My God, we're going to pay so desperately for this,* but instead, "My father called and congratulated me. He said, 'What took you so long?'"

The *New York Daily News* headline about the uprising was both obnoxious and accurate: Homo Nest Raided, Queen Bees Are Stinging Mad. "We had discovered a power that we weren't even aware that we had," recalled Danny Garvin, another rioter. "All of a sudden, I had brothers and sisters . . . which I didn't have before."

But not everyone shared that family feeling. Perry Brass watched the riot from a distance with one of his wealthier gay friends, who fumed. "'It'll blow our cover,' [the] Ivy League graduate pronounced. 'Everything was so good for us. We had our bars, our beaches, our restaurants. Now the girls have blown all that.'"

▲ ▼ ▲

"You have to give them hope. Hope for a better world, hope for a better tomorrow..."
—Harvey Milk

5

Into the Streets

1970s

June 28, 1970 ▶ People started gathering in Sheridan Square around noon—about 25, tops. Craig Rodwell, one of the organizers of the Christopher Street Liberation Day march, was worried. Police had blocked off the square to keep the expected crowd from spilling out into the street, yet with so few people, the barricades hardly seemed necessary.

But then groups started arriving—East Coast chapters of the Daughters of Bilitis and the Mattachine Society; local organizations, like the Gay Activist Alliance and the Lavender Menace; college clubs; and plenty of curious onlookers, though many of them lingered some distance away. In all, maybe a thousand people had gathered.

◀ **"Harvey's Human Billboard" during his unsuccessful 1975 campaign for the San Francisco Board of Supervisors.** Harvey Milk Archives—Scott Smith Collection, Gay & Lesbian Center, San Francisco Public Library

Ten minutes after 2 PM, police ordered Rodwell to get the march started—they didn't have all day. Parade marshals were armed with flyers to pass out along the route. They said, in part, "The Christopher Street Liberation Committee has worked closely with the New York City Police Dept. and we have received their full cooperation to ensure an orderly and successful march." Rodwell thought it was funny. This parade was in honor of the first anniversary of the Stonewall Uprising, a riot where the police were on the losing end. And now the cops were *protecting* the people who battled against them? Crazy!

In the first few blocks, the nervous participants walked quickly—people later joked that it was more of a "run" than a "march." Some carried posters that said FREE OSCAR WILDE, GAY POWER, and HI MOM! As they headed north up Sixth Avenue, something happened: bystanders left the sidewalks and joined the parade, egged on by marchers who chanted, "Out of the closets and into the streets!" The crowd doubled, then doubled again. By the time the first marchers reached Central Park fifty blocks away, there were 5,000 more behind them (and some say as many as 15,000), stretching back fifteen blocks.

The happy crowd poured out into Sheep Meadow near the south end of the park. Many scaled a granite outcropping to look back at those still arriving. "For all of us who had been slowly climbing for years toward our freedom, this one last hill which let us look across our dear brothers and sisters was a cup running over," wrote Robert Liechti. "It was as if . . . now at last we had come to the clearing, on the way to the top of the mountain, . . . and tho' we knew we still had far to go, we were moving, and we knew it."

Other parades were held the same weekend in Los Angeles, Chicago, and San Francisco. It had been a busy year, and the 1970s had just begun.

▼ ▲ ▼

Losing That Wounded Look

LESS THAN a week after Stonewall, on July 4, 1969, forty New York gay activists boarded a chartered bus for Philadelphia and the Annual Reminder outside Independence Hall. The organizers were expecting a fair amount of media attention—the deputy mayor of Philadelphia and his wife were scheduled to join the picketers.

The demonstration started as all others had—men and women marching single-file in a circle, silent, serious, and behaved. But then two women joined hands. Frank Kameny, who was directing the protest, ran up to the couple.

"You can't do that! You can't do that!" he scolded, then slapped their clasped hands.

The New York delegation, who made up the majority of the picketers, felt the pair certainly could "do that." After briefly huddling, they returned to the picket line with new slogans written on their posters. They'd crossed off EQUALITY FOR HOMOSEXUALS and written SMASH SEXUAL FASCISM! Others joined hands. It was as much a message to Kameny as to the confused tourists who watched. Clearly, Kameny had to get with the program he helped start— or get out of its way.

In the months following Stonewall, there was a major shift in the gay rights movement. Allen Ginsberg saw it the weekend of the uprising—"They've lost that wounded look," he told a friend.

Just after the riots, the Mattachine Society painted a message on the boarded-up front window of the Stonewall Inn: WE HOMOSEXUALS PLEAD WITH OUR PEOPLE TO PLEASE HELP MAINTAIN PEACEFUL AND QUIET CONDUCT ON THE STREETS OF THE VILLAGE—MATTACHINE. But very few people in the LGBT community were interested in peace and quiet.

The Gay Liberation Front

ON JULY 9, a meeting was held in New York to plan a Gay Power Vigil to protest police harass-

ment. It would be held in Washington Square Park, one month after the Stonewall riot. On July 27 Marty Robinson addressed the 200 or so people who came: "Let me tell you homosexuals, we've got to get organized. We've got to

The Gay Liberation Front marching on Times Square, fall 1969. Photo by Diana Davies. Manuscripts and Archives Division, The New York Public Library

stand up." Martha Shelley agreed, and added: "The time has come for us to walk in the sunshine. We don't have to ask permission to do it. Here we are!"

Later that summer, a group of peace activists and breakaway Mattachines formed the Gay Liberation Front, or GLF. "[It] became a community fast," recalled Jerry Hoose, an early member, "because we were so angry."

Some, like Morty Manford, thought it looked exciting:

I was sitting with some friends having a sandwich at Mama's Chick 'n' Rib, a coffee shop on Greenwich Avenue popular with gay people, when a demonstration went by. Hundreds and hundreds of people with protest signs were chanting. It was obviously a gay demonstration. I said to my friends at the table, "Let's join it," Nobody wanted to join it, and I said, "I'll see you later." I wasn't going to let the parade go by.

"It was like fire.... People were ready," Jim Fouratt recalled, "We wanted to *end* the homophile movement. We wanted them to join *us* in making a gay revolution." Barbara Gittings, who had been working on LGBT rights for more than a decade, was stunned. "Would you believe, the gay liberation people called us on the carpet during the meeting and asked us to explain who we were and what we were doing there at a GLF meeting?"

One of GLF's first actions was to host a "Coming Out Dance." Tickets were $1.50. Visibility was the goal. Over the next year, dances spread to campuses across the nation, and 40 college chapters were launched. There were even GLF chapters in Montreal, Vancouver, and London.

On November 14, 1969, GLF began publishing a newspaper, *Come Out!*, after the *Village Voice* refused to accept advertisements and meeting notices that contained the word "gay." (The paper later reversed its policy after GLF picketed its offices, which were just a few doors down from the Stonewall Inn.)

"Every day brought something new, something challenging," said the GLF's Néstor Latrónico. "Meetings, demonstrations, consciousness-raising groups.... The atmosphere was exhilarating. The world felt new, as if it had just been created."

The Gay Activist Alliance

NOT EVERYONE in the gay liberation movement was a fan of GLF—it was a chaotic organization where almost every idea brought forth in a meeting, no matter how kooky or poorly thought out, was discussed late into the night. GLF only survived nine months, but it launched the community down the path of activism and confrontation.

In late December 1969, Jim Owles, Marty Robinson, Arthur Evans, and others started a new organization, the Gay Activist Alliance (GAA), which had narrower goals and ran its meetings according to *Robert's Rules of Order*. Members had to attend three meetings before they were allowed to participate. GAA would focus on issues specific to the LGBT community, not build bridges to the Black Panther Party or protest the war raging in Vietnam. (Both were on GLF's very long agenda.)

With community building in mind, in 1970 GAA purchased an old firehouse at 99 Wooster Street in Manhattan's SoHo neighborhood. It was used as a community center for meetings and Saturday night "Liberation Dances."

Upstairs, volunteer Vito Russo began showing "Firehouse Flicks," rare old movies with LGBT characters, to larger and larger crowds. Movie nights were almost as popular as the dances, and eventually took over the dance floor on Friday nights. "[There] were all these gay people in the audience watching these films and we discovered that we all laughed at the same places," remembered Arthur Evans.

"The experience of seeing those movies with an almost all-gay audience was quite different from seeing them in mainstream theaters," Russo noticed. "It also seems like gay audiences

The GAA Firehouse, 1971.
Photo by Diana Davies. Manuscripts and Archives Division, The New York Public Library

are always pulling for the underdog." He became an expert on Hollywood's portrayal of the LGBT community, and later wrote an important book, *The Celluloid Closet*.

The Celluloid Closet

Vito Russo loved movies, but he loved the LGBT community even more. And he understood how closely they were connected. "People were being taught things about us as gay people that simply weren't true," he said, "and they were being taught these things by mass media, by movies." Not only that, films affected how LGBT people thought about *themselves*. After all, when nearly every gay or lesbian seen on film was a criminal or crazy or doomed to a life of loneliness and eventual suicide, what would you expect people to think?

Russo made it his mission to educate the public. Throughout the 1970s, he spoke to packed theaters across the United States, where he showed film clip examples of what he'd learned. His book, *The Celluloid Closet*, took seven years to research and three years to write, and it was rejected by 18 publishers before it came out in 1981. The book was so popular it was expanded and updated six years later, and was later made into a film documentary.

Vito Russo, circa 1981. HBO/Photofest, © HBO

STAR

Sylvia Rivera and Marsha P. Johnson were outside the Stonewall Inn the first night of the uprising. Some say Johnson threw the first rock, though a lot of people claimed credit for that. Seventeen-year-old Rivera joined in as well. "I'm not missing a minute of this—it's the revolution!" she told her friends.

Rivera and Johnson were both transgender and part of the LGBT street culture—young homeless runaways, often kids thrown out by their families, who lived on the streets of America's gay neighborhoods, like Greenwich Village. And though they had helped launch the gay liberation movement, they were often ignored by the rest of the community. Or worse.

But Rivera and Johnson weren't the type to be ignored. If they didn't have the support of the gay and lesbian mainstream, they would go off on their own. In 1970 they started the Street Transvestite (later changed to Transgender) Action Revolutionaries, better known as STAR, to fight for transgender rights and to help youth who were living on the street. They turned an abandoned building on New York's Second Street into a shelter for runaways: STAR House.

"When we asked the community to help us, there was nobody to help us. We were nothing. We were nothing!" Rivera recalled. "Marsha and I were young and we were taking care of kids that were younger than us."

STAR would continue to be at the forefront of the gay liberation movement, whether some in the movement wanted it or not. "You people run if you want to, but we're tired of running," one of STAR's leaflets read. "We intend to fight for our rights until we get them."

Zap!

ONE OF the first strategies used by the Gay Activist Alliance (GAA) to raise the public's awareness of homophobia—hatred or fear of LGBT people—was the "zap." GAA members would show up at press conferences, society gatherings, television tapings, or anywhere there was a large crowd or an open mic, and when everyone least expected it, they would hijack the event for as long as they could.

"The idea was, these are like little theatrical productions," recalled Arthur Evans. "We knew we could create these little scenes for TV, so we'd go out and get arrested and then we'd come home and watch it on TV." (Vito Russo also videotaped many of the zaps to show at the firehouse.) Zaps weren't polite, they weren't especially profound, but they did get attention. And results. And they were fun.

New York mayor John Lindsay, who had promised a meeting with gay rights groups

Under the umbrella, Sylvia Rivera (left) and Marsha P. Johnson at a protest outside New York city hall, April 1973. Photo by Diana Davies. Manuscripts and Archives Division, The New York Public Library

but never delivered, was the zappers' first target. On April 13, 1970, Lindsay was speaking on the steps of the Metropolitan Museum of Art for its 100th anniversary when Marty Robinson walked up, leaned into his microphone, and asked, "When are you going to speak out on homosexual rights, Mr. Mayor?" Security dragged Robinson away, but soon others were asking—shouting, actually—the same question from out in the crowd.

From then on, whenever Lindsay appeared in public, GAA was there. They zapped him at fundraisers. They zapped him at ribbon-cuttings. They zapped him on television shows and at Radio City Music Hall. They even zapped him at the base of the Metropolitan Opera House's grand staircase on opening night. When he finally decided he'd had enough, Lindsay asked Eleanor Holmes Norton, chairperson of the New York City Commission on Human Rights, to sit down with GAA and others to address the problem of employment discrimination in the city.

GAA quickly learned that the media appreciated a good show. Vincent Gillen, founder of a private investigation agency called Fidelifacts, once explained how the company gathered information on suspected gay employees: "I like to go on the rule of thumb that if one looks like a duck, walks like a duck, associates only with ducks, and quacks like a duck, he is probably a duck." So Marty Robinson put on a white duck costume and showed up outside Gillen's office with other GAA protesters.

Marty Robinson certainly *looked* like a duck at the Fidelifacts zap, January 18, 1971. Photo by Rich Wandel, courtesy LGBT Community Center National History Archive

The newspapers loved it. However, when the media itself was being zapped, they were less amused.

Challenging the Media

IN OCTOBER 1970 *Harper's* magazine published an essay by Joseph Epstein in which he claimed he wanted to "wish homosexuality off the face of this earth." Early one morning a few weeks later, GAA appeared at the magazine's offices with a large urn of coffee and a platter of breakfast snacks. "Good morning," they'd announce as each person arrived, "*I'm* a homosexual. We're here to protest the Epstein article." Then they'd point to the buffet. "Would you like some coffee? Cream and sugar? Pamphlet? Have a donut." After a day-long sit-in and discussion with GAA, *Harper's* agreed to "open channels to the gay community."

Nobody escaped the zap, not even TV anchorman Walter Cronkite. On December 11, 1973, fourteen minutes into the *CBS Evening News*, activist Mark Allan Segal jumped between Cronkite and the camera with a handwritten sign that read, GAYS PROTEST CBS PREJUDICE, then sat down on Cronkite's desk. Sixty million people were watching the live broadcast, which quickly went blank.

In the studio, technicians and producers tackled Segal and tied him up with video cables. Three minutes later, after they'd pulled him into the hallway, the broadcast resumed. "Well, a rather interesting development in the studio here: a protest demonstration right in the middle of the CBS News studio," Cronkite began. "The young man was identified as a member of something called Gay Raiders, an organization protesting alleged defamation of homosexuals on entertainment programs."

Segal, who had posed as a college reporter to get into the studio, was charged with second-degree criminal trespassing and went on trial in the spring. Walter Cronkite was called as a witness. During a pause in the trial, he approached Segal and asked why he did it.

Segal wasn't shy: "Your news program censors," he stated. "If I can prove it, would you do something to change it?" Cronkite made no promises, but listened. Segal gave three examples of recent biased stories, one about the New York City Council rejecting a gay rights ordinance for a second time, which Cronkite wrote. "Why haven't you reported on the 23 other cities that have passed gay rights bills?" Segal asked.

Cronkite thanked Segal and promised to think about what he said. Segal was found guilty and fined $450—he was caught on camera, after all. But later he got a call from Cronkite, asking to meet about the network's coverage of LGBT issues. Within a month, CBS

SYMBOLIZE THIS

THE LOWERCASE Greek letter lambda, λ, has been a symbol of the gay rights movement since the early 1970s. It was suggested by Tom Doerr of GAA because lambda indicated "a complete exchange of energy" in chemistry and physics. The gender symbols ♂ and ♀, drawn from the planetary symbols for Mars and Venus, were also paired together to symbolize same-sex couples. In 1993, Holly Boswell created a new symbol to represent the transgender community:

And today, the logo of the Human Rights Campaign, the largest LGBT civil rights organization in the United States, is an equal sign.

Look at the following list of symbols and the concepts they often represent.

Greek Letters: α (alpha—first or beginning), Δ (delta—change), Ω (omega—last or final)

Planetary Symbols: ☉ (Sun), ⊕ (Earth), ☽ (Moon), ♄ (Saturn), ♆ (Neptune)

Mathematics: +, −, ×, ÷, =, <, >

Common Symbols and Punctuation: $, ¢, &, ♫, ?, !

Emoticons: :-), :-o

Now design a logo for your favorite cause that uses one of these symbols, or a symbol or letter you find somewhere else, such as from the Hebrew alphabet or Egyptian hieroglyphs. What font, color, or background shape should you use? Can you create a logo that uses a combination of symbols? You can create the logo freehand, on paper, or you can use a computer.

broadcast a report on ten US cities that had recently passed gay rights ordinances, all labeled on a great big map.

Cronkite made coverage of gay and lesbian issues a regular feature on his broadcasts. He and Segal became lifelong professional friends, with Segal becoming CBS's informal advisor on LGBT stories. Segal even joined the media, and in 1976 began publishing the *Philadelphia Gay News*. Years later, recalling the zap, he admitted that the fine he paid was "the happiest check I ever wrote."

Gay Marriage in the Heartland

ACROSS THE nation, gays and lesbians were joining the fight for LGBT civil rights. The first challenge to the ban on same-sex marriage came in Minneapolis, Minnesota. On May 18, 1970, Jack Baker and his partner, Mike McConnell, walked into the Hennepin County Courthouse and asked for a marriage license.

"This is not a gimmick," Baker told the clerk. "We really want to do it. A homosexual ought to have equal rights, privileges, and responsibilities." The clerk turned them away, claiming the county attorney had said "to permit two males to marry would result in an undermining and destruction of the entire legal concept of our family structure in all areas of law."

The rejection was the least of their troubles. McConnell had been offered a job at the University of Minnesota Library shortly before he and Baker had asked for a marriage license. The university withdrew the offer and told him not to show up to his first day of work.

McConnell sued the school, and won. A "homosexual is after all a human being, and a citizen of the United States," Judge Phillip Neville wrote. "He is as much entitled to the protection and benefits of the laws and due process fair treatment as are others." Ordered to rehire McConnell, the university appealed the decision to a higher court. That court reversed the decision, and the ruling stood after the US Supreme Court refused to hear the case. McConnell never regained the job.

Two months after McConnell and Baker were turned down in Minnesota, another couple applied for a marriage license in Louisville, Kentucky. On July 7, 1970, Tracy Knight and Marjorie Ruth Jones were denied a license by James Hallahan, the clerk of Jefferson County, who said their union could "lead to a breakdown in the sanctity of government," and worried, "it could spread all over the world!"

The couple sued, and were treated with even less respect at the trial. Judge Landon Schmid wouldn't even start the proceedings until Tracy Knight changed out of her beige pantsuit and put on a dress. "She is a woman, and she will dress as a woman in this court," he explained. Later, when the judge could find no Kentucky law specifically preventing the two women from marrying, he used the definition of marriage from *Webster's New International Dictionary* to prop up his ruling.

Despite these setbacks, gay couples started marching into other county clerks' offices around the nation—in Tampa, Florida; Hartford, Connecticut; Chicago, Illinois; Milwaukee, Wisconsin; and New York City. All were turned away.

Then, back in Minnesota, McConnell and Baker tried to get married again. And this time, it worked! Jack Baker had legally changed his name to Pat Lynn McConnell, and the clerk in the Mankato office where they sent the application just assumed Pat Lynn was a woman's name. With a marriage license in hand, the pair turned to Pastor Roger Lynn, a Methodist minister, who pronounced them "husband and husband" on September 3, 1971.

Lynn signed their marriage certificate and submitted it to the state. A short film of the ceremony was mailed to the media, and it was reported worldwide. The newlyweds then sat back and waited for the state to bring a lawsuit.

A month later, the Minnesota Supreme Court ruled against the couple for their *first* attempt to marry. In 1972 the Hennepin County Attorney tried to get a court to nullify their

Michael McConnell (left) and Jack Baker, 1970.

Photo by Kay Tobin. © Manuscripts and Archives Division, The New York Public Library

Jeanne Manford's poster from the 1972 Christopher Street Liberation Day Parade.

second marriage license, but never made it to a judge. The state decided to simply ignore the marriage altogether. In 2011, Baker and McConnell celebrated their 40th anniversary together.

Parents, Families, and Friends of Lesbians and Gays

WHEN SCHOOLTEACHER Jeanne Manford got the news that her adult son Morty was in the hospital after being assaulted at the New York Hilton, she was more angry than afraid.

Morty had been at New York's Inner Circle Dinner. The annual banquet was a gathering of local reporters and city officials, and GAA was there protesting the media's unfair treatment of the LGBT community. Morty was handing out flyers when he was punched, kicked, and shoved down an escalator by Michael Maye, the president of the city firefighters' union, as police stood idly by.

Jeanne Manford called the *New York Times* and demanded that it investigate the violence that had occurred under its reporters' noses. They hung up on her. So Manford wrote a letter to the *New York Post*, and the paper published it on April 29, 1972. She proclaimed, "I am proud of my son, Morty Manford, and the hard work he has been doing in urging homosexuals to accept their feelings and not let the bigots and sick people take advantage of them in the ways they have done in the past and are continuing to do."

That June, Morty invited his mom to march with him in the Christopher Street Liberation Day Parade. She agreed, as long as she could carry a picket sign. Manford's hand-printed sign read, PARENTS OF GAYS: UNITE IN SUPPORT FOR OUR CHILDREN.

A First

ON MARCH 7, 1972, East Lansing, Michigan, became the first city in the United States to enact an antidiscrimination ordinance protecting gays and lesbians from being fired from their jobs. The law had been suggested and pushed by the Gay Liberation Movement, a student organization at Michigan State University. After the city council voted 4–1 in favor of the law, GLM's founder Don Gaudard reminded the press, "Not everything happens in San Francisco."

The crowd went bonkers. Manford received hugs and kisses and cheers all along the parade route—even she was surprised at the reaction. Manford got so many requests to speak to other parents that on March 11, 1973, along with her husband, Jules, she hosted a new support group titled Parents of Gays at Manhattan's Metropolitan-Duane United Methodist Church. About 20 people attended.

The Manfords' movement grew to include family members and friends, and took on the name Parents and Friends of Lesbians and Gays—PFLAG—and later Parents, Families and Friends of Lesbians and Gays. Today the organization has more than 350 chapters in the United States and abroad.

We're Not Sick

WITH THE Annual Reminders a thing of the past, Frank Kameny and Barbara Gittings decided to throw most of their efforts into reforming the psychiatric community. To do this, they would have to change the *Diagnostic and Statistical Manual of Mental Disorders*—usually called the *DSM*.

First published in 1952, the *DSM* was (and still is) the main tool used by psychiatrists to treat patients. And despite Dr. Evelyn Hooker's research, in 1970 the *DSM* still listed homosexuality as a mental disorder. Doctors routinely acted as if gays and lesbians could be "cured."

So in 1970 Kameny, Gittings, GAA, and several doctors disrupted the annual meeting of the American Psychiatric Association (APA). They challenged a psychiatrist who used electric shocks on his gay patients, and later danced at the closing banquet—men with men and women with women. Realizing this was an issue it would need to address, the APA agreed to have a panel—"Lifestyles of Non-Patient Homosexuals"—at its next meeting in Washington, DC.

Frank Kameny volunteered to speak on behalf of the gay community, to tell the doctors what people like him had been through. When the day came, Kameny waited offstage at the hotel ballroom with the rest of the panel, including several esteemed psychiatrists who wore gold medals around their necks. Meanwhile, GAA members were sneaking in the stage's back doors, ready to zap. When the doctors realized what was about to happen, Kameny said, they "beat our people over the head with their gold medals and . . . drove them out the door."

"I realized something had to be done," Kameny recalled. "I marched across the room, stepped up on the stage, and the psychiatrist in charge said, 'What are you doing?' and I said, 'I'm going to speak.'" Somebody cut off the microphone, so Kameny loudly announced, "[You] may take this as a declaration of war against you." The APA meeting quickly adjourned.

Many APA members also wanted change. A group calling itself the Committee of Concerned Psychiatrists was already lobbying its members to throw out the *DSM* diagnosis. However, they needed to be in leadership positions to do so. In 1972 they ran a new slate of candidates in the APA election and swept out every last old officer, medals and all.

At the same conference, the APA heard from a gay psychiatrist (and army veteran) who testified under the pseudonym Dr. H. Anonymous at a panel titled "Psychiatry: Friend or Foe to Homosexuals?" His real name was John Fryer, but he wore a wig and a mask and used a microphone that distorted his voice. "In those days gay psychiatrists were not out. Period," said Kameny. Fryer's personal story changed many members into believers—the old diagnosis had to go.

At APA's 1973 conference in Hawaii the attendees heard even more presentations from gays and lesbians. Later, in December, APA's leaders voted unanimously to remove homosexuality from the list of disorders in the *DSM*. A Philadelphia newspaper's headline announced: Twenty Million Homosexuals Gain Instant Cure.

Some of the old doctors protested. Many had made their careers trying to "cure" gays. The board's decision had been rigged, they said, and they demanded that every APA member be allowed to vote on the subject at its 1974 meeting. They did: 58 percent voted to keep homosexuality out of the *DSM*, with only 38 percent wanting it reinstated.

The Lavender Menace

WHEN FEMINIST Betty Friedan convened the First Congress to Unite Women in November 1969, one group of women was not on the list of sponsors: the Daughters of Bilitis. Friedan was the president of the National Organization for Women, better known as NOW, and believed that the feminist movement was in danger of being taken over by its lesbian members—a "lavender menace" she told the *New York Times Magazine*.

Many of the early gay liberation groups weren't much kinder to lesbians—white men usually dominated the leadership, as well as the agendas. At Gay Liberation Front dances, said writer Ellen Shumsky, "There were so many men . . . that the women felt lost to each other. It was intolerable to many, but the women put up with it, hoping it would change."

"Enough already," Rita Mae Brown finally told a GLF meeting in January 1970. "We can't

Barbara Gittings, Frank Kameny, and Dr. H. Anonymous at the 1972 APA convention. Photo by Kay Tobin. © Manuscripts and Archives Division, The New York Public Library

be out in NOW, the guys dominate this, we need a lesbian feminist civil rights movement. Come to my house Wednesday night." About 30 women showed up, and they devised a plan.

Moments after the *Second* Congress to Unite Women started on May 1, 1970, somebody turned out the lights in the auditorium. When they came back on, Rita Mae Brown, Martha Shelley, and 15 others were standing on stage wearing purple T-shirts that said LAVENDER MENACE and TAKE A LESBIAN TO LUNCH. Most of the 400 or so women in the crowd cheered and welcomed the activists into the meeting. But not everyone was happy—Friedan later told the *New York Times* that she believed some of the protesters were CIA operatives.

This new group called themselves the Radicalesbians. At the congress they passed out the "Woman-Identified Woman" manifesto, a ten-paragraph paper about why lesbians were so important to the women's movement. "What is a lesbian?" the manifesto started. "A lesbian is the rage of all women condensed to the point of explosion."

Other lesbian groups soon joined the effort: the Furies Collective from Washington, DC; Gay Women's Liberation from San Francisco; Lesbian Feminist Liberation (LFL), originally known as the Women's Subcommittee of the New York GAA; and many more.

As active participants in the 1970s women's movement, lesbians helped create new institutions just for women, such as women's health organizations, magazine and book publishers, concerts and music festivals, and more. Other groups, like Combahee River Collective, formed in Boston in 1974, addressed the needs, issues, and concerns of African American lesbians.

Rita May Brown (front right) at the Lavender Menace protest, May 1970. Photo by Diana Davies. Manuscripts and Archives Division, The New York Public Library

There was also a separatist movement within the lesbian community. It grew out of separatist feminism, women who chose to focus strictly on the rights of women and girls, and wanted nothing to do with male-dominated society.

Infighting

THE LGBT civil rights movement also began to see a growing divide between the lesbian and transgender communities.

The rift first became public at the 1973 West Coast Lesbian Feminist Conference. After it was announced that singer Beth Elliot would be performing, some tried (unsuccessfully) to get her taken off the program because she was male-to-female transgender. They believed she could not fully relate to other women because of her assigned sex at birth. Many of the attendees were fine with Elliot being there, but a vocal group tried to shout her down when she was on stage.

A similar quarrel took place on June 24, 1973, at New York's Christopher Street Liberation Day. At a rally in Washington Square Park after the parade, Sylvia Rivera pushed her way onto the speakers' platform. Rivera told the crowd to move the protest to the city's detention center, but she got booed off the stage. Jean O'Leary, leader of the LFL, then took the microphone to criticize an earlier drag performance, saying it was demeaning to women.

Vito Russo tried to calm the crowd. "Listen to her! You listened to everyone else! Listen! That's the least we can do for each other!" he begged. When O'Leary finished, another unannounced speaker took the stage. Lee Brewster, a leader in the drag community, angrily reminded the crowd that they had been on the front lines at the Stonewall Uprising.

Just when things were at their worst, Russo pulled his friend Bette Midler up onto the platform and shoved a microphone in her hand. *Sing!!* She launched into her familiar song, "Friends," and by the time she hit the chorus, many had joined in.

> *But you got to have friends!*
> *The feeling's oh so strong.*
> *You've got to have friends,*
> *To make the day last long!*

The crowd calmed, but not much—some of the angriest people had already left.

In a way, the LGBT civil rights movement was a victim of its own success. In the beginning, there were barely enough people to even argue. Now, with so many people coming out and joining the struggle, they were discovering how different they all were. It was only natural that they would have different ideas and different goals.

To many outside the movement, however, gays, lesbians, and transgender men and women were still all the same. And they didn't like any of them, not one bit.

New Battlegrounds

WITH THE LGBT community making great advances in the early 1970s, it was probably inevitable that there would be a backlash. Had the movement been too demanding? Too rude?

Truth was, there were still many people who would never support LGBT rights no matter how nicely anyone asked. And when it came to being rude, gays and lesbians were nothing compared to Anita Bryant.

The trouble started after the Dade County Board in Miami, Florida, passed a civil rights ordinance on January 18, 1977. It was the first gay rights law to pass in the South, and made discrimination based on sexual orientation in housing, employment, and public accommodations—restaurants, hotels, and stores—illegal. Anita Bryant, a singer, former Miss Oklahoma, and spokesperson for the Florida Citrus Commission, stepped up as the face of a new conservative organization: Save Our Children.

"As a mother, I know that homosexuals cannot biologically produce children; therefore, they must recruit our children," she claimed, hoping to get frightened parents to support

LGBT Hero — **Leonard Matlovich (1943–1988)**

On September 8, 1975, Leonard Matlovich became the first openly gay person to appear on the cover of *Time* magazine. A veteran of the US Air Force, Matlovich volunteered for three tours in Vietnam, earned the Bronze Star, and received a Purple Heart after he stepped on a land mine. But in early March 1975, he told his commanding officers that he was gay, and after a review by a military panel, he was discharged as "unfit for duty," despite his spotless record.

Matlovich had been working with Frank Kameny and others to challenge the Pentagon's ban on gays and lesbians. Matlovich sued. In 1978 a federal court ordered him returned to duty with back pay, but the government appealed. Two years later, in an out-of-court settlement, the US Air Force upgraded his dismissal to an "honorable discharge" and gave him $160,000 in back pay. But he never returned to his career as a technical sergeant.

Matlovich died of AIDS on June 22, 1988, and was buried in Washington's Congressional Cemetery. His headstone reads:

Never Again, Never Forget
A Gay Vietnam Veteran
When I was in the military
they gave me a medal for killing two men
and a discharge for loving one.

repealing the law. Bryant said she spoke for the "normal majority" and stated "if gays are granted rights, next we'll have to give rights to prostitutes and to people who sleep with St. Bernards and to nailbiters."

Bryant's cruel campaign worked. On June 7 voters repealed the new law by a 70 to 30 percent margin. The day after the election, the Florida legislature passed another law banning gays and lesbians from adoption, as well as a law banning same-sex marriage (even though it was still illegal in all states at that point). And in the weeks to follow, many LGBT employees around Miami were fired.

Encouraged by her success, Bryant decided to take her crusade to other cities. The following year, St. Paul, Minnesota; Wichita, Kansas; and Eugene, Oregon, all repealed their gay rights ordinances, with campaigns funded in part by Anita Bryant Ministries and her Save Our Children organization.

The antigay forces were on a roll. Next, they set their sights on the nation's most populated state: California. State Senator John Briggs authored a ballot measure known as Proposition 6, which mandated that all gay and lesbian teachers be fired. Also, any teacher could be dismissed for "advocating, imposing, encouraging, or promoting" LGBT issues in the public schools.

"Homosexuals want your children," Briggs claimed. "If they don't recruit children or very young people, they'll all die away. They have no means of replenishing. That's why they want to be teachers."

Early polls predicted that Proposition 6 would pass easily, and Bryant gave Briggs her list of supporters to finance the campaign. But John Briggs, who wanted to be the state's next governor, underestimated a newly elected city supervisor from San Francisco, Harvey Milk.

The Mayor of Castro Street

ON APRIL 1, 1974, the residents of Ann Arbor, Michigan, elected Kathy Kozachenko of the Human Rights Party to the city council. Less than a year later, voters in Massachusetts sent

Signs protesting against Anita Bryant at the 1977 San Francisco Gay and Lesbian Freedom Day Parade. Harvey Milk Archives—Scott Smith Collection, Gay & Lesbian Center, San Francisco Public Library

Elaine Noble to the state senate. Both local elections made national news because both women were open lesbians, the first "out" candidates to take public office in the United States.

Had Harvey Milk won the first time he ran for the San Francisco Board of Supervisors, he would have been the first. But he lost his election in 1973. And 1975. And 1976, when he ran for the California state assembly.

But by 1977, Harvey Milk had learned a lot about politics. Over the years, he had stitched together a partnership of LGBT voters, union members, African Americans, Latinos, Asian Americans, the elderly, and small business owners in the city's largely gay Castro District. (It was referred to as "the Castro" and some called Milk the "Mayor of Castro Street" for organizing the annual street fair.) Milk cut off his ponytail and mustache and put on a second-hand suit. He was ready for a fourth campaign.

The campaign was run out of the back room of Milk's camera shop. "We had volunteers in all different shapes and sizes, from [11-year-old] Medora Payne . . . up to 70-year-old women who wanted to be doing something—maybe they couldn't be walking the precincts but they wanted to do something for Harvey," remembered Anne Kronenberg, Milk's campaign manager. "It was a nice mix of people."

There were 16 other candidates running against him, but when the ballots were counted

Sydney Mardi Gras Attack

ON **JUNE 24, 1978,** the Australian LGBT community wanted to honor the Stonewall Uprising with a march through Sydney. After a day of political rallies demanding the government put an end to discrimination, about 2,000 people paraded through the city streets.

The police had other plans. After blocking the marchers, they began beating and arresting them. "There was . . . pretty serious bashing and kicking and all sort of things going on," recalled protester Diane Minnis. "It was a real riot."

Fifty-three people were arrested. Demonstrators surrounded the Darlinghurst police station where those arrested were being held, and even more people were taken into custody. Before the protests were over, 184 people had been put behind bars. Though charges were dropped against the original 53, their names were run in local papers, and some lost their jobs.

A Mardi Gras parade was organized in Sydney for the following year to commemorate the uprising started by an uprising, and has been held every year since. Today, it draws more than 350,000 participants.

on November 8, Milk had gotten more votes than anyone else—30 percent. The Castro went wild. "It was more than just a candidate winning," said Kronenberg. "It was the fact that all these lesbians and gay men throughout San Francisco who had felt like they'd had no voice before now had someone who represented them."

The day he took office, Milk walked to work from the Castro with his supporters. "You can stand around and throw bricks at Silly Hall," he said when he arrived. "Or you can take it over. Well, here we are." He tackled many issues, including voting machines, downtown development, rent control, taxes, and a pooper scooper law. But one of his proudest achievements was passing a long-overdue gay rights ordinance banning discrimination in housing, public accommodations, and the workplace. Only one city supervisor voted against it: Dan White.

"No On 6"

HARVEY MILK had been in office just a few months when Proposition 6 was announced, and he found himself thrust into a leadership role to defeat the measure, though more than 30 different organizations were already working against it. Most in the LGBT community read the early polls with dread: newspapers reported that almost twice as many people supported Prop 6 as opposed it.

The "No On 6" campaign started in the gay community. "My name is Harvey Milk, and I want to recruit you," Milk told the crowd at the 1978 Gay Freedom Day Parade. "I want to recruit you for the fight to preserve your democracy from the John Briggs and the Anita Bryants who are trying to constitutionalize bigotry."

The campaign borrowed a slogan from *The Wizard of Oz*: "Come Out! Come Out! Wherever You Are!" They encouraged LGBT citizens to talk to their families, friends, and coworkers to let them know the personal damage the law would do. If a person voted for Prop 6, it was a vote against their neighbors, their brothers and sisters, their children.

Harvey Milk (right hand raised) walked from the Castro to city hall with his supporters on his first day of work, January 9, 1978. Photo by Daniel Nicoletta

Harvey Milk fires up the crowd at the Christopher Street Liberation Day rally in Los Angeles, 1978. Photo © Pat Rocco, all rights reserved

Barbara Jordan (1936–1996)

Unlike Harvey Milk, most LGBT politicians were not out of the closet during the 1970s, though they were still passionate advocates for human rights. Elected to the US House in 1972, Texas Representative Barbara Jordan became the first African American woman in Congress from the South. She is best known for her role in the 1974 impeachment hearings for President Richard Nixon. And in 1976 Jordan gave the keynote address to the Democratic National Convention.

Many expected Jordan to run for higher office—senator, or perhaps even president—but she left public service in 1979 after being diagnosed with multiple sclerosis. She spent her remaining years teaching at the University of Texas and living a private life with her partner, Nancy Earl. She was awarded the NAACP's Spingarn Medal in 1992 and the Presidential Medal of Freedom in 1994.

Library of Congress (LC-DIG-ppmsc-01268)

"No On 6" then sent tens of thousands of volunteers door-to-door to tell their stories. "Lesbian separatists worked with men; street people with stockbrokers," Gayle Wilson, a Los Angeles activist recalled. "People who would hardly speak with each other learned to set aside their own goals—and their anger—to work together."

The campaign even gained some unexpected allies. Conservative former governor Ronald Reagan came out against Prop 6 and wrote an op-ed for the *Los Angeles Herald-Examiner*: "Whatever else it is," he said, "homosexuality is not a contagious disease like the measles. Prevailing scientific opinion is that an individual's sexuality is determined at a very early age and that a child's teachers do not really influence this."

By Election Day in November, the tide had turned. Prop 6 was defeated by a 42 to 58 percent margin, and lost in every single California county. Even better, a ballot measure called Initiative 13 was defeated in Seattle the same day. It would have cancelled the city's antidiscrimination ordinance, but it lost 37–63.

In a celebration on election night, Milk told a joyous crowd, "To the gay community all over this state, . . . so far a lot of people joined us and rejected Proposition 6, and now we owe them something. We owe them to continue the education campaign that took place. We must destroy the myths once and for all—shatter them!" Then Milk told them how:

Most importantly, every gay person MUST come out! As difficult as it is, as hard as it is, you must tell your immediate family. You must tell your relatives. You must tell your friends if, indeed, they are your friends. You must tell your neighbors. You must tell the people you work with. You must tell the people in the stores you shop in. And once they realize we really are their children, and we are indeed everywhere, every myth, every lie, every innuendo will be destroyed once and for all. And once you do, you will feel so much better.

Tragedy at City Hall

THREE WEEKS after the victory over Proposition 6, Harvey Milk was dead. On November 27, 1978, supervisor Dan White entered city hall and shot Mayor George Moscone four times. Then he walked down the hall to Milk's office

LGBT Hero **Tom Ammiano (1941–)**

When he came out as gay to his coworkers in 1975, Tom Ammiano was taking a huge risk. Ammiano was an elementary teacher in the San Francisco Unified School District, and wanted to protest the lack of job protection for gay and lesbian teachers. He was the first California teacher to publically come out, and he picketed the district's board meetings alongside other educators. Finally, on June 17, 1975, the board voted unanimously to add protections for LGBT teachers. Ammiano would join Harvey Milk and others to found the "No On 6" campaign three years later.

After many years of teaching and community activism, Ammiano ran for a seat on the San Francisco School Board in 1990, and won. Four years later was elected its president. In 1994 he won a seat on the San Francisco Board of Supervisors. He served for fourteen years, including four years as board president. In 2008 he ran for California State Assembly, and won. He currently represents California's Assembly District 17, which includes the eastern half of San Francisco.

Photo courtesy California Assembly

and shot him five times. Both men died at the scene.

San Franciscans responded to the tragedy that evening with a peaceful candlelight vigil. Thousands marched from the Castro down Market Street to city hall where they joined even more mourners. "I think we sent a message to the nation that night, about what our immediate response was: not violence, but a certain respect for Harvey and a deep, deep regret and feeling of tragedy about it," reflected Sally Gearhart, a college professor who had worked with Milk in the "No On 6" campaign.

Earlier that evening, several hours after killing Moscone and Milk, Dan White turned himself in at a local police station with his wife by his side. Some of the officers greeted him as if he was a hero.

Why did he do it? White had been elected to the Board of Supervisors the same year as Harvey Milk. A former police officer and fireman, he claimed to represent "traditional values" and the non-gay, non-minority voters of San Francisco. But on November 10, 1978, after not even a year in office, White resigned. He said he couldn't afford to raise his family on a supervisor's salary. Then, five days later, he said he wanted his job back. The mayor refused.

On the day of the murders, Dan White crawled through a side window of city hall to avoid the metal detectors. He calmly went to the mayor's office and asked to meet with Moscone. Once he was inside, they argued, and White shot Moscone. White reloaded, walked down the hall, and killed Milk before he even got out of his chair.

It looked like two premeditated, first-degree murders. Still, many in the city's police

ACTIVITY
DESIGN A FLAG

THE RAINBOW FLAG everyone knows today was created by artist Gilbert Baker. The first rainbow flag appeared in San Francisco's Gay Freedom Day Parade on June 25, 1978.

The original design had eight stripes, where each stripe had a different meaning: pink for sexuality, red for life, orange for healing, yellow for sunlight, green for nature, turquoise for art, blue for harmony, and violet for spirit. You will notice, however, that today's rainbow flags have only *six* stripes. That's because it became difficult to find inexpensive cloth in pink and turquoise.

You'll Need
▶ Sheet of white paper
▶ Colored pencils or markers
▶ Construction paper or colored cloth

Now it's your turn. If you could design a flag for your school or club or city or state, what would it look like? Keep in mind how difficult it would be to produce—the more complicated it is, the more expensive it will be.

Start by drawing your design on a sheet of white paper using colored pencils or markers. Once you have your flag design, create a small version out of construction paper or, with adult help, sew it with cloth.

department rallied behind White, who they saw as one of their own. They helped raise $100,000 for a Dan White Defense Fund, and some wore FREE DAN WHITE T-shirts.

At White's trial, gays, lesbians, and racial minorities were prevented from serving on the jury. White's defense attorneys painted him as a family man under incredible stress, mistreated by the mayor. They said he wasn't thinking clearly, his brain confused by eating too much junk food. Attorney Douglas Schmidt told the jury, "Good people, fine people with fine backgrounds, simply don't kill people in cold blood. It just doesn't happen."

But clearly it *had* happened. Reporters joked about the so-called "Twinkie defense" and said it wouldn't work, but they were wrong. On May 21, 1979, the all-white, all-straight jury found Dan White guilty of only two counts of voluntary manslaughter (a much lesser charge than first-degree murder).

The gay community erupted. Supervisor Harry Britt, appointed to Milk's seat after the murders, stood before the TV cameras. "Harvey knew that the lowest nature of human beings would rise up and get him—but he never imagined the city would approve of that act. It is beyond immoral—it is obscene!"

Within hours, a mob descended on city hall chanting "Avenge Harvey Milk!" and "We Want Justice!" and "Kill Dan White!" LGBT leaders linked arms, trying to keep the police and protesters apart, but the cops clubbed them and hauled them away. Rioters smashed windows and set fire to a dozen squad cars lined up along the street.

Later that night, the San Francisco police showed up in the Castro District looking for revenge. Decked out in riot gear with black

Burning squad cars outside San Francisco city hall during the White Night Riots, May 21, 1979.

Photo by Daniel Nicoletta

tape covering their badges (to prevent identification), they clubbed people on the streets at random, then chased a crowd into the Elephant Walk Bar, which the cops then destroyed. By sunrise, 60 police and 100 protesters had been taken to the hospital. The events became known as the White Night Riots. No police were ever charged in the assaults, and the LGBT community did not apologize.

Dan White was sentenced to seven years in prison. He served five. The LGBT community, which made up 20 to 25 percent of the city's voters, later took out its anger at the ballot box. Every member of the Board of Supervisors but Harry Britt lost his or her seat in the next election. So did the district attorney, who many in the community believed had bungled the White prosecution.

Some of the final words on Milk's murder were had by Harvey himself. He knew he could be the target of a crazed homophobe, so he left a tape recording with his will. "If a bullet should enter my brain," he said, "let that bullet destroy every closet door."

A Meeting and a March

BACK IN the 1960s, Frank Kameny was outside the White House, protesting. On March 26, 1977, he was inside as an invited guest. A few months earlier, Jean O'Leary of Lesbian Feminist Liberation had been talking to Midge Costanza, an advisor to President Jimmy Carter. "I think it's time gay people stopped picketing the White House on the outside," O'Leary said. "I think it's time to ask for a meeting on the inside. What do you say?"

Costanza said yes! The meeting between the new administration and the 14-person delegation was the first ever summit between the White House administration staff and the LGBT community. It was held on a Saturday when President Carter was outside Washington. O'Leary, Kameny, Elaine Noble, Troy Perry, Charlotte Spitzer of PFLAG, and others had a talk with staff in the Roosevelt Room. They talked about LGBT discrimination and tax law and military service and healthcare and immigration and on and on and on—three hours' worth.

Fourteen people having a meeting with the president's advisors was certainly a major accomplishment, but in Washington, few things get political attention without big numbers. People are power. So the LGBT community began planning a march on the nation's capital. Just before he was murdered, Harvey Milk had suggested the idea. A year later, it happened.

On October 14, 1979, about 75,000 American citizens went to Washington, DC, for the first National March on Washington for Lesbian and Gay Rights. Chanting "We Are Everywhere!"

The National March on Washington for Lesbian and Gay Rights, with the Washington Monument in the background, October 14, 1979.

they called for a federal bill on lesbian and gay rights that included changes to adoption rules, the right to serve in the military, protections for LGBT youth, and an end to discrimination in employment, housing, and public accommodations.

"For us the feeling of being there and marching in the nation's capital was amazing—the sense of community, of solidarity. And the numbers of people!" recalled Penelope Tzougros. "The whole experience was phenomenal because for the first time in our lives it felt like we were in the majority."

It had been a remarkable decade for the LGBT community, filled with victories and heartaches. And nobody knew that soon there would be a threat that would challenge them as never before.

▲ ▼ ▲

AR

> "Act Up!
> Fight Back!
> Fight AIDS!"
>
> —ACT UP protest chant

6

AIDS and a Conservative Backlash

1980s

July 3, 1981 ▶ The story appeared in the *New York Times*: RARE CANCER SEEN IN 41 HOMOSEXUALS:

> *Doctors in New York and California have diagnosed among homosexual men 41 cases of a rare and often rapidly fatal form of cancer. Eight of the victims died less than 24 months after the diagnosis was made. . . .*

◀ **Artist Keith Haring created posters used by ACT UP.** ACT UP New York Records, Manuscripts and Archives Division, The New York Public Library, Astor, Lenox, and Tilden Foundations, © Keith Haring Foundation

©K·Haring 89

IGHT AIDS
ACT UP

The sudden appearance of the cancer, called Karposi's Sarcoma, has prompted a medical investigation. . . .

In a letter alerting other physicians to the problem, Dr. Alvin E. Friedman-Kien of New York University Medical Center, one of the investigators, described the appearance of the outbreak as "rather devastating." . . .

Dr. Friedman-Kien said he tested nine of the victims and found severe defects in their immunological systems.

The article ran on page 20, deep enough into the paper that a reader could miss it. But many in the gay community didn't miss it, and were shocked. Few if any could have imagined that this outbreak would turn into a plague that would infect and kill thousands, then millions worldwide.

▼ ▲ ▼

Fighting for Their Lives

LARRY KRAMER read the *New York Times* article that day. He was not a gay activist at the time. "Like many others, when Gay Pride marches started down Fifth Avenue at the end of June, I was on Fire Island. Gay politics had an awful image. Loudmouths, the unkempt, the dirty and unwashed," he later admitted. "On Fire Island, we laughed . . . when we watched the evening news on Sunday night flash brief seconds of those struggling, pitiful marches."

Kramer was an author and screenwriter with many friends in the gay community. A few of those friends—still young men—had recently and unexpectedly died. *Could they have contracted this new disease?*, he wondered. Kramer contacted Dr. Lawrence Mass, and then Dr. Friedman-Kien, and soon realized he had to do something. Quickly.

Kramer and several friends called a meeting at his apartment on August 11, 1981, just six weeks after the *Times* article. "Eighty men sat down with Dr. Friedman-Kien who told us in no uncertain terms exactly what was happening." For some reason, gay men were dying from a rare form of skin cancer, Karposi's Sarcoma, as well as *Pneumocystis carinii* pneumonia. Lab tests showed the patients' immune systems, which would normally fight off these diseases, were severely damaged. And nobody knew why.

The August meeting raised $6,635 and launched the Gay Men's Health Crisis (GMHC), the first organized response to the AIDS crisis. (AIDS is an acronym for acquired immunodeficiency syndrome.) Soon after, Californians created the San Francisco AIDS Foundation and the AIDS Project Los Angeles. These organizations would, in time, provide medical information, counseling referrals, food, legal advice, companionship, dog walking, housecleaning, and even funeral arrangements for those hit with HIV (human immunodeficiency virus), the virus that causes AIDS.

Two weeks after that first meeting, Kramer made an appeal to the New York LGBT community in the *New York Native*, a gay newspaper:

I hope you will write a check and get your friends to write one, too. This is our disease and we must take care of each other and ourselves. In the past we have often been a divided community; I hope we can all get together on this emergency, undivided, cohesively, and with all the numbers we in so many ways possess.

The article was direct, but Kramer was polite. His tone would soon change.

Negligence and Denial

IT WAS more than a year after the AIDS crisis began before it was even mentioned by an official in President Reagan's administration. A reporter questioned Deputy Press Secretary Larry Speakes at a press briefing on October 15, 1982:

Question: *Larry, does the president have any reaction to the announcement—the Centers for Disease Control in Atlanta, that AIDS is now an epidemic and have over 600 cases?*

Speakes: *What's AIDS?*

Q: *Over a third of them have died. It's known as "gay plague." (Laughter.) No, it is. I mean it's a pretty serious thing that one in every three people that get this have died. And I wondered if the president is aware of it?*

Speakes: *I don't have it. Do you? (Laughter.)*

Q: *No, I don't. . . .*

Speakes: *How do you know? (Laughter.)*

Q: *In other words, the White House looks on this as a great joke?*

Speakes: *No, I don't know anything about it, Lester.*

Q: *Does the president, does anybody in the White House know about this epidemic, Larry?*

Speakes: *I don't think so. I don't think there's been any—*

Q: *Nobody knows?*

Speakes: *There has been no personal experience here, Lester.*

Reagan administration officials had no excuse for not knowing more about AIDS. The US Centers for Disease Control (CDC) and the National Institutes of Health (NIH) were under their control. The fact is, they *did* know there was an epidemic. They just didn't care.

Larry Kramer with Molly, 1989. Photo by Robert Giard, courtesy Estate of Robert Giard

"There is no doubt in my mind that if the same disease had appeared among Americans of Norwegian descent, or among tennis players, rather than gay males, the responses of both the government and the medical establishment would have been different," said California Representative Henry Waxman, chair of the House Energy and Commerce Subcommittee on Health and the Environment. One of his subcommittee's first actions was to give $2 million to the NIH to study AIDS. The NIH had only asked for $1 million. Some in the gay community began saying that NIH stood for Not Interested in Homosexuals.

And if the government was guilty of inaction, so were many in the LGBT community. "People were acting out of their denial. . . . The first reaction was to simply avoid dealing with the disease," said Randy Shilts, a gay reporter with the *San Francisco Chronicle*. Shilts was routinely criticized by gay leaders for reporting honestly about the AIDS crisis. Many didn't want to hear the bad news, or to change their behavior. HIV, which causes AIDS, is spread mainly through sexual contact.

Back in New York, Larry Kramer realized that if anything was going to change, it was going to have to come from the people most at risk. Gone were the days of polite appeals for money and volunteers. On March 14, 1983, Kramer wrote a famous open letter to the gay community, "1,112 and Counting," which ran in the *New York Native*:

> *If this article doesn't scare the shit out of you, we're in real trouble. If this article doesn't arouse you to anger, fury, rage, and action, gay men may have no future on this earth. Our continued existence depends on just how angry you can get. . . .*
>
> *After almost two years of an epidemic, there still are no answers. After almost two years of an epidemic, the cause of AIDS remains unknown.*

He went on to criticize the Reagan administration, New York mayor Ed Koch, the medical establishment, and the *New York Times*. But he saved much of his anger for the gay community, who he felt was sitting back, waiting for somebody else to solve the problem, or denying that it even was a problem. Kramer ended the essay by listing the names of twenty men he knew that had already perished, and finished, "If we don't act immediately, then we face our approaching doom."

And then, following the open letter, was a two-paragraph announcement: VOLUNTEERS NEEDED FOR CIVIL DISOBEDIENCE. It began, "It is necessary that we have a pool of at least three thousand people who are prepared to participate in demonstrations of civil disobedience," and ended, *"Start these lists now."*

On Their Own

AS THE AIDS crisis worsened, the LGBT community started to rally, putting aside the disagreements that had driven them apart in the 1970s. They had little choice. For the most part, they were on their own, abandoned by parents and family, neighbors and coworkers, and the government.

Even the medical community was terrified by AIDS. Many doctors, nurses, and hospital staff avoided patients. Some refused to enter the same rooms with the sick. But others stepped up. "When straight nurses didn't want to work in AIDS wards, lesbian nurses did," recalled Torie Osborn, a Los Angeles organizer. "They *wanted* to do it." Lesbians, who had experience fighting for their own medical issues, became vocal leaders in the fight. Activist Robin Tyler recalled lesbians "talking about how they'll never talk to a man again in the 1970s, and there they were pushing the wheelchairs, making the hospital visits, changing guys. And so history brought us back together. This historic happening of AIDS."

By October 1983 the GMHC was the leading health provider for AIDS patients in New York City. According to Larry Kramer, "Over 400 patients [were] supervised by over 300 trained clinical volunteers each and every day. . . . Over 1,500 Hotline phone calls [were] logged every week.... Over 2 million pieces of printed literature giving the most up-to-date information [were] dispatched all over the world."

Without the US government's assistance or approval, LGBT doctors and AIDS activists also worked to identify new experimental drugs from other countries. They then smuggled these drugs into the United States and distributed them through underground (and illegal) "buyers clubs." Most of these new treatments turned out to be useless, or even harmful. But what choice did patients have? They had to try something.

Attacking the Victims

As THE LGBT community struggled with the AIDS crisis, its critics and enemies used it as an opportunity to attack. "I don't think that there's new bigotry or new homophobia," said Vito Russo. "I think this is the same homophobia, but AIDS has given people permission to say it out loud."

And they did. Rev. Jerry Falwell of the Moral Majority proclaimed, "AIDS is not just God's punishment for homosexuals, it's God's punishment for the society that tolerates homosexuality." A group calling itself Dallas Doctors Against AIDS said "the citizenry of this country [should] do everything in their power to smash the homosexual movement in this country." Conservative columnist William F. Buck-

ley wrote an editorial in the *New York Times* advocating the tattooing of "all AIDS carriers."

Buckley's outrageous suggestion reminded many of what happened during the Holocaust. So did a 1986 California ballot initiative pushed by millionaire Lyndon LaRouche, Proposition 64. The "LaRouche Initiative" was placed on the ballot by his Prevent AIDS Now Initiative Committee—PANIC. If passed, it would mandate HIV testing, bar HIV-positive individuals from working in food service jobs or with children, and even quarantine them in camps. The proposition was defeated by a 71–29 percent margin, but only after opponents spent millions on the "No On 64" campaign, money that would have been better spent on AIDS research and health services.

It wasn't just crackpots like Lyndon LaRouche attacking the LGBT community—mainstream political and religious leaders joined in the bashing. On October 1, 1986, the prefect of the Roman Catholic Church, Joseph Cardinal Ratzinger (who in 2005 would become Pope Benedict XVI) issued the *Letter to the Bishops of the Catholic Church on the Pastoral Care of Homosexual Persons*. In it he wrote that those who are gay have a "tendency toward an intrinsic moral evil," and that "when civil legislation is introduced to protect homosexual behavior... neither the Church nor society at large should be surprised when... irrational and violent reactions increase."

A picket sign used in a protest against the Moral Majority. Courtesy Gay, Lesbian, Bisexual, Transgender Historical Society

Even the LGBT community's allies weren't at their best. "One of the saddest lessons I have learned from this epidemic is that the true heterosexual liberal, for some unaccountable reason, is not necessarily the gay person's friend," wrote the always-blunt Larry Kramer. "He or she will fight for blacks, women, Hispanics, abortion, nuclear disarmament, keeping the Jefferson Library open all week. But when it comes to homosexuality, they get queasy."

Not All Bad News

BECAUSE AIDS occupied so much of the LGBT community's attention during the 1980s, it was sometimes easy to miss small but important victories being made in gay civil rights. Yet in 1982 Wisconsin became the first state to pass a law banning gay and lesbian discrimination statewide. By the early 1980s, about 120 corporations had adopted nondiscrimination policies covering sexual orientation, including AT&T and IBM. And on December 5, 1984, Berkeley, California, became the first city to offer benefits to domestic partners, just as it already did for spouses of married employees.

In Washington, the Gay Rights National Lobby, which was formed in 1976, became the Human Rights Campaign Fund in October 1980. Later dropping the word "Fund," HRC is today the largest LGBT civil rights and political lobbying organization in the United States.

March Controversy

IN 1983 THERE WAS AN UPROAR surrounding a celebration honoring the 20th anniversary of the March on Washington for Jobs and Freedom, where Martin Luther King had given his famous "I Have a Dream" speech. The National Coalition of Black Gays had asked to participate in the program but were blocked by DC Congressman Walter Fauntroy, a member of the Coalition of Conscience organizing the rally. "If we have somebody speaking about gay rights," he said, "then we might as well have someone speak about penguin rights."

Angered LGBT activists reminded the organizers that the original 1963 march had been organized by an openly gay man, Bayard Rustin (see page 59). But the committee wouldn't budge. Then some in the coalition, like the National Organization for Women and the American Friends Service Committee, threatened to pull out. Activists also had a sit-in at Fauntroy's office.

Finally, lesbian feminist poet Audre Lorde was given a spot in the program. Rev. Joseph Lowery, who had worked with King during the Montgomery Bus Boycott, spoke out: "Twenty years ago we marched, and one year later, the 1964 Civil Rights Act was passed. It is now time to amend that act to extend its protections to lesbians and gay men." Coretta Scott King then announced that she believed the protections of the 1964 Civil Rights Act should be extended to gays and lesbians.

Lorde's speech at the 20th anniversary celebration addressed the controversy. "We know we do not have to become copies of each other in order to be able to work together. We know that when we join hands across the table of our difference, diversity gives us power. When we can arm our selves with the strength and vision from our diverse communities, then we will in truth, all of us—be free at last!"

And in late summer 1982, more than 1,300 athletes gathered in San Francisco for the first Gay Games. Organized by former Olympic athlete Dr. Tom Waddell, it included 17

THE HIGH FIVE

HAVE YOU EVER given somebody a high five? The very first high five was between baseball players Glenn Burke and Dusty Baker on October 2, 1977. Baker had just hit his 30th home run of the season, and his L.A. Dodgers teammate met him at home plate, his right hand high over his head. Baker and Burke slapped hands, and the high five was born. Burke then hit a home run of his own.

Glenn Burke was out to his teammates, but didn't tell the public he was gay until after his 1979 retirement. Still, he was the first pro baseball player to do so. Burke later moved to San Francisco's Castro District, where he would greet friends with a high five. Residents soon used the greeting as a way to express gay pride.

Can you come up with a handshake or greeting that is unique to your group—your sports team, classmates, or friends? It could be a secret shake or an elaborate ritual with many steps.

different events, including volleyball, swimming, boxing, cycling, and track and field. The Gay Games are still held every four years, and since 1994 have attracted more participants than the Winter Olympics.

The amateur participants at the Gay Games weren't the only athletes to come out of the locker room closet. Starting in the 1970s, professional athletes began coming out as well. In 1975 David Kopay, who had played football for several National Football League teams before retiring in 1972, became the first pro athlete to say he was gay. In 1982, Major League Baseball outfielder Glenn Burke came out as well.

Many of the first open LGBT athletes were tennis players. Renée Richards, who had undergone sex-reassignment surgery in 1975, sued to compete in the US Open tennis tournament as a woman. She won the court case and earned the right to enter the tournament, but she lost on the tennis court—she was defeated in her first match. Tennis superstar Billie Jean King was forced out of the closet during a bitter lawsuit in 1981. Martina Navratilova also came out in 1981, but by her own choosing.

Creating New Families

EVEN IF they never wanted to come out, AIDS was forcing many in the gay community out of the closet. For some, revealing they had the virus also meant acknowledging they were gay to their friends, family, and coworkers. And those people who did not have the virus could not be blind to the discrimination faced by their friends and loved ones. More and more people felt that it was important to come out, and did.

As people came out, or were forced out, many were fired from their jobs and disowned by their families. Worse still, their LGBT families, who had stood by them, were often pushed aside. Spouses, partners, and friends were turned away at hospitals, unable to visit their loved ones. If a person died, his or her life savings and belongings were turned over to their biological families, even if they no longer spoke to one another, while their surviving gay partners got nothing and were sometimes tossed out of homes they had built together.

When Leslie Blanchard died of AIDS on September 14, 1986, his partner of ten years, Miguel Braschi, was told to leave the couple's New York apartment. Only Blanchard was listed on the lease—he had been renting the apartment since before meeting Braschi. The men were all but legally married at the time Blanchard died, and Blanchard gave most of his estate to Braschi in his will. The owner of the apartment, Stanley Stahl, didn't care—he wanted Braschi out.

Rather than leave, Braschi sued Stahl. After a three-year court battle the New York Court of Appeals ruled that the couple's relationship was "familial." In other words, they were essentially a married couple—a family—even though they couldn't be married under state law. The ruling was a big step forward in LGBT civil rights.

Meanwhile, during the 1980s, a quiet revolution was taking place: lesbian couples were having children. New medical procedures meant more options for women hoping to start families.

And with children came new legal problems they'd never considered before. Could two women be listed as mothers on a birth certificate? Usually not. If the couple later broke up, as did half of all heterosexual marriages, how would custody work? Would the biological mother be given primary custody? Usually so. (For gay men, the legal hurdles for adoption and surrogacy were even more difficult.)

Helping LGBT Youth

IN NOVEMBER 1983, the Institute for the Protection of Gay and Lesbian Youth opened in New York City with a $50,000 donation from a closeted gay man. It was designed to help teens who were struggling to understand their sexuality. Some were runaways or had been thrown out of their families for being gay, lesbian, bisexual, or transgender. Others were still living with their families, but had no one like themselves to talk to.

"I remember a 12-year-old boy from the Bronx who would call me up once a week just to talk and ask questions about being gay," recalled social worker Joyce Hunter. "He wanted to talk to another gay person. We'd also talk about a whole bunch of things, like his schoolwork." But at least that kid had a home. "A good percentage of our kids are thrown out on the street by their parents," Hunter said. "We had one young man who was a throwaway from Boston. He came from a close-knit Italian

NASA

LGBT Hero: Sally Ride (1951–2012)

At 7:33 AM on June 18, 1983, the Space Shuttle *Challenger* launched into orbit from Cape Canaveral. Five astronauts were aboard, including mission specialist Sally Ride. During the six-day mission, Ride launched a satellite using the Shuttle's robotic arm and carried out numerous experiments. She also became the first American woman in space, as well as the youngest American in space (a record that still stands).

Ride would return to orbit once more in October 1984, again aboard the *Challenger*. After leaving NASA she founded Sally Ride Science to develop science material for middle-grade students. Not until she died from pancreatic cancer on June 23, 2012, did the public learn that Tam O'Shaughnessy, with whom she had written six books, had been her partner for 27 years. A year after her death, Ride was awarded the Presidential Medal of Freedom. O'Shaughnessy accepted it on her behalf.

family. He thought he could share his being gay with them.... They threw him out of the house. He never went home. But he had us."

In April 1985, the Institute opened the Harvey Milk High School for LGBT youth. It was a small school—just 15 students in a classroom set up in the back of the office. It was open to students who were having difficulty with harassment and bullying in their home schools, usually because of their sexual orientation. At Harvey Milk, students could express themselves more openly without fear of violence or intimidation.

An Unexpected Ally

THOUGH THE AIDS crisis had been raging for four years, the issue didn't "hit" the American public until actor Rock Hudson revealed he had the disease. Hudson had become popular in the 1950s playing romantic leading men, so it was a shock to many that he was both gay and HIV positive.

Hudson came out in the summer of 1985 and died that autumn, on October 2. Just two weeks earlier President Reagan, who had been a friend of Hudson's, uttered the word AIDS in public for the first time. By then, 15,000 people had already died from the disease. Reagan was asked about the crisis at a news conference. He claimed his administration had requested more than $500 million of AIDS research. But

that wasn't true—they hadn't even asked for half that amount. Reagan was claiming credit for the US Congress, which had approved more aid than Reagan had put in his budget.

It wasn't until October 1986 that somebody in the administration seemed to take the crisis seriously. Surgeon General C. Everett Koop issued a blistering report that asked for increased funding and, most of all, public education. Up until that moment, only the struggling LGBT community had been working on safe-sex education campaigns. Koop's report said,

Many people, especially our youth, are not receiving information that is vital to their future health and wellbeing because of our reticence in dealing with the subject of sex, sexual practices, and homosexuality. This silence must end. We can no longer afford to sidestep frank, open discussions about sexual practices—homosexual and heterosexual. Education about AIDS should start at an early age so that children can grow up knowing the behaviors to avoid to protect themselves from exposure to the AIDS virus.

Koop had been appointed to his position by Reagan in 1981, but was told for five years that he could not speak publically about the epidemic. He even tried several times to speak *privately* with the president and his advisors, but they never would. This, however, is the Surgeon General's main job as the nation's chief public health educator. Koop also saw it as his personal duty. "My position on AIDS was dictated by scientific integrity and Christian compassion," he said.

Frustrated, Koop tried to force the president's hand: "We [had] to embarrass the administration into bringing the resources that [were] necessary to deal with this epidemic forcefully." But Reagan was embarrassed only far enough to *appear* to be doing something. It was around Thanksgiving 1987, with 25,644 people already confirmed dead, that he announced the administration was going "to determine as soon as possible the extent to which the AIDS virus has penetrated our society."

Reagan's Presidential Commission on the HIV Epidemic did not have its first meeting until late 1987. Some members of the group understood the epidemic, but many were uninformed and even hostile to the LGBT community. One member thought a person could become infected by sitting on a toilet seat; another had called gay people "blood terrorists." California Representative Henry Waxman said that many panel members were chosen "because they know nothing about AIDS or had already made up their minds to go along with the right-wing agenda rather than a public health agenda in dealing with the disease."

Six years into the epidemic, and this was the best the government could do? AIDS sufferers and the LGBT community realized they would need to try another approach. Something much louder.

Bowers v. Hardwick

DURING THE darkest days of the AIDS crisis, the US Supreme Court delivered a punch to the gut of the LGBT community. On June 30, 1986, the court ruled in *Bowers v. Hardwick* that gay and lesbian Americans had no constitutional right to their intimate personal lives. They were second-class citizens.

The *Bowers v. Hardwick* case began in 1982. Michael Hardwick had been arrested by an Atlanta policeman who had entered his apartment. The policeman found Hardwick in bed with another man, which under Georgia law could land him in prison for 20 years. When prosecutors realized the officer had entered Hardwick's home illegally—he didn't have a valid warrant—they dropped the charges. Nevertheless, Hardwick filed suit and it took almost three years before the case made it to the nation's highest court.

Writing to support the 5–4 majority decision, Chief Justice Warren Burger stated that the Georgia law against people of the same sex having sex was "firmly rooted in Judeo-Christian moral and ethical standards" and

Surgeon General C. Everett Koop, circa 1982.
United States Public Health Service

GO ON A RIBBON HUNT

IN 1991 PEOPLE BEGAN wearing small red ribbons on their lapels to raise awareness of AIDS and express compassion and support for those who suffered from the disease. Visual AIDS, the organization that came up with the idea, chose red because of its "connection to blood and the idea of passion—not only anger, but love, like a valentine." Since then, ribbons of many colors have been used—some say overused—to bring attention to various causes.

Now it's time for a Ribbon Hunt. How many different colored ribbons can you find? Has anyone in your family worn a ribbon for a cause? Have you seen ribbons on cars, in advertisements, or at charity walks or events? What colors are they, and what do they symbolize? (Here's a hint to get you started: Think pink.) Keep a list of all the ribbons you find—once you start looking, you'll find more than you expect.

that to overturn it would "cast aside millennia of moral teaching." It didn't matter if Hardwick and his partner were in the privacy of their own home—they were still breaking the law.

Justice Harry Blackmun strongly disagreed. "This case is about 'the most comprehensive of rights, and the right most valued by civilized men,' namely 'the right to be left alone,'" he wrote in his dissent, also saying that he hoped the court would one day reverse itself.

The LGBT community didn't want to wait for "someday." Just hours after *Bowers* was announced, 600 people marched in San Francisco. The following day, a thousand LGBT protesters held a rally in New York's Sheridan Square near the Stonewall Inn. They blocked traffic on Seventh Avenue for three hours, chanting "1-2-3-4, civil rights or civil war!" and singing "We Shall Overcome." And at a protest outside the Supreme Court in Washington, Jeff Levy of the National Gay and Lesbian Task Force said, "Every time they knock us down, whether it's the Justice Department or the Supreme Court or Anita Bryant in the '70s, we come back even stronger than before."

Other rallies were held in cities like Cincinnati, Ohio, and Dallas. On July 4, President Reagan and Chief Justice Burger came to New York to celebrate Liberty Weekend and were greeted by 6,000 shouting marchers at Battery Park. "We have a message for Burger, we have a message for Falwell, we have a message

for Reagan," thundered organizer Darrel Yist. "The message is: 'We've had enough and we're not going to take it anymore.'"

ACT UP!

ANGER OVER the *Bowers* decision and the government's behavior during the AIDS crisis sparked a new wave of activism in the LGBT community. A group calling itself the Lavender Hill Mob, organized by the GAA's former leader Marty Robinson and his friends, held an old-style zap at an event honoring Chief Justice Burger. Later they protested at a CDC conference on AIDS, disrupting a press conference of LGBT organizations by shouting, "You've sold out the gay community!"

But Larry Kramer really got things rolling on March 10, 1987. It happened at a gathering at the Lesbian and Gay Community Services Center in New York. Kramer had long since burned his bridges at the Gay Men's Health Crisis—he wanted them to take on the politicians who were doing nothing, and the GMHC was more focused on assisting those already infected by HIV. And not making waves.

"Turn on the lights. I have things to say," Kramer began, then detailed how bad things had gotten. "Four years ago, there were 1,112 cases of AIDS nationwide. There are now officially—and we know how officials count—32,000 with 10,000 of these in New York." He pointed to a large section of the audience and asked them to stand. "At the rate we are going, you could all be dead in less than five years. Two-thirds of this room could be dead in less than five years."

On and on he went, and it was grim. Kramer singled out the Food and Drug Administration (FDA) for his greatest criticism. It was taking too long to approve new experimental drugs and treatments. He ended with a call to action. "Every one of us here is capable of doing something. Of doing something strong. We have to go after the FDA—fast. This means coordinated protests, pickets, arrests. Are you ashamed of being arrested?"

Apparently not. After he finished speaking, the crowd of 250 scheduled a planning meeting for two days later. Three hundred people showed up, and before the evening was over they founded the AIDS Coalition to Unleash Power—ACT UP. Chapters soon popped up across the nation. Kramer, Marty Robinson, and Vito Russo were some of its early leaders, but others stepped into leadership roles, like Ann Northrup. "At ACT UP I found a great working democracy that was very positive and supportive of everybody," she recalled.

ACT UP didn't waste time. They planned a March 24 protest on Wall Street against the FDA and Burroughs Wellcome, the drug company that was charging patients $10,000 a year for the AIDS medicine AZT, one of the most expensive drug treatments ever known. About 250 men and women staged a "die-in," where they collapsed in the street and didn't move, and 17 were arrested. The protesters hung an effigy (a life-sized figure) of Dr. Frank Young, the FDA's administrator, in front of Trinity Church, handed out more than 10,000 protest flyers, and tied up traffic in lower Manhattan for several hours. They also succeeded in getting coverage on every nightly television newscast, as well as in newspapers coast to coast.

One of ACT UP's flyers ended up in the hand of Peter Staley, who happened to be passing the protest on the way to work. Staley was a closeted, gay, Wall Street bond trader, and he was HIV positive. And frightened. "It [was] like living in a war. All around me, friends [were] dropping dead, and you're scared for your own life all at the same time." But the protest impressed him, and he made a big decision: "I said, 'Enough of this. This job is going to kill me.' So, I went on disability and decided to become a full-time AIDS activist."

Iris Long was also attracted by the early ACT UP protests. She was a retired research chemist living with her husband in nearby Queens. And while she was impressed by ACT UP's dedication, she quickly realized that the group did not understand how the government's medical bureaucracy worked. According to Kramer, Long confronted the group at a meeting: "You guys don't know diddly about what this is, and

ACT UP protesters weren't just ready to be arrested, they bragged about it. Author's collection

ACT UP wanted the world to know about President Ronald Reagan's negligence during the AIDS crisis. Grany Fury Collection, Manuscripts and Archives Division, The New York Public Library, Astor, Lenox, and Tilden Foundations

[In the image:]
This Political Scandal Must Be Investigated!
54% of people with AIDS in NYC are Black or Hispanic... AIDS is the No. 1 killer of women between the ages of 24 and 29 in NYC... By 1991, more people will have died of AIDS than in the *entire* Vietnam War... What is Reagan's *real* policy on AIDS? Genocide of all Non-whites, Non-males, and Non-heterosexuals?... SILENCE = DEATH

anybody who wants to learn about the system, how it works, how grants are made, how the science works, how *everything* works, how the NIH works, how the FDA works, how you can deal with this enormous amount of material. I'll teach you." And she did.

ACT UP put every one of its volunteers to use. A group of artists and advertising experts created posters and stickers and flyers, many bearing the group's famous, simple logo: a pink triangle, from the Holocaust, over the line Silence = Death.

Marches, NAMES, and Coming Out

In 1985, as they had every November 27 since 1977, San Franciscans held a candlelight memorial to honor Harvey Milk. Before the march, activist Cleve Jones had asked everyone to write the names of people they knew who had died of AIDS on pieces of white cardboard. Jones feared that nobody was documenting those who had, in a sense, vanished. The names were later taped to the federal Health and Human Services office building in protest.

That night, staring up at the panels, Jones had a memory of his grandmother's quilt back in Indiana. It inspired Jones and his friends to plan a permanent memorial to those lost to the disease. In February 1987 the first three-by-six-foot

panel—by design, roughly the size of a grave—was created in memory of Marvin Feldman. The NAMES Project Foundation (NAMES is an acronym for National AIDS Memorial Education and Support) was established that June, and in time the NAMES Quilt it created would become the largest community art project in the world.

AIDS groups across the nation began contributing panels of their loved ones, which were collected in NAMES's San Francisco storefront. The goal was to bring the quilt to the Second National March on Washington for Lesbian and Gay Rights in October 1987.

Some would call it "The Great March"—650,000 people came to the nation's capital to demand more from their government, and their fellow citizens. On October 10, 1987, the day before the march, 2,000 couples participated in a marriage ceremony outside the IRS building. And then, on the cold autumn morning of October 11, the NAMES Quilt was unfurled on the National Mall. It had 1,920 panels and was larger than two football fields—almost two city blocks. "It was like . . . lotus flower after lotus flower after lotus flower, and each petal was a person," recalled Guy Clark, a florist from San Francisco. "It was so powerful. You didn't have to say anything—the tears would just come."

"I didn't understand what it was until I actually walked onto the field, and saw. And started to walk around, and see also the reaction of other people who were looking at the panels," said Barbara Gittings. "I think [it] is one of the most inspired ideas of the Twentieth Century."

At the end of the day, the march ended with a plea to everyone who had been there to come out. To their families, their neighbors, and their coworkers. The following October 11, the one-year anniversary of the march, was designated as National Coming Out Day. But the marchers weren't quite finished. Two days later, 571 protesters were arrested at the Supreme Court building, carted off by Capitol Police wearing rubber gloves. Michael Hardwick, whose legal case had caused so much outrage, was one of those arrested.

As important as the 1987 march was, the nation's three largest news magazines—*Time*, *Newsweek*, and the *US News and World Report*—didn't bother to report that it had taken place.

Yet it had. And it mattered. Between 1985 and 1994, the number of Americans who claimed to have a gay friend or close acquaintance rose from 22 percent to 43 percent—it almost doubled. People were coming out, and more would follow.

A year after the march, in October 1988, the NAMES Quilt returned to Washington. This time, 8,288 panels were spread out on the Eclipse, a grassy oval just south of the White House. President Reagan could see it easily from the Oval Office.

REMEMBER A LOVED ONE WITH A QUILT PANEL

HAVE YOU EVER LOST A LOVED ONE? How would you remember your family member or friend with a quilt panel? You do not have to sew an actual cloth panel—a drawing could be just as nice.

You'll Need
► 1 sheet of paper
► Ruler
► Colored pencils or markers
► Cloth, fabric paint (optional)

Start by creating a smaller-scale version of a 3-by-6-foot panel. Basically, the drawing should be twice as long as it is wide. (For a standard sheet of paper, start with a rectangle that is 10 inches long and 5 inches wide.)

Think about what you want to show. The panel should include the loved one's name, but everything else is up to you. What was important in that person's life? What do you remember most fondly about him or her? Use colored pencils or markers to decorate the panel.

If you plan to actually create a 3-by-6-foot cloth panel, think about how it will be constructed. Will you sew or glue pieces of fabric onto the panel? Or use paints? Or both? Some NAMES panels use personal items as part of the design, like a favorite T-shirt. Others have photographs attached. You will probably need an adult's help to build the final panel. This is a great opportunity to share your memories of a loved one as you work on it together.

And if you would like to make a panel for the actual NAMES Quilt, you can still do so. Find instructions for creating and submitting your panel at www.aidsquilt.org/make-a-panel. The organization also asks that you send a letter about the person you are memorializing.

© SomSak Kham Kula

The NAMES Quilt at the 1993 March on Washington. Photo by author

Fight Back!

FOR YEARS, AIDS activists had basically replaced the services they weren't getting from their own government. They had been caregivers, researchers, and even smugglers of new experimental drugs from around the world. ACT UP's Iris Long finally put her foot down. *This is your government. You're taxpayers. You're citizens. Don't go around them. Make the FDA, the CDC, and the NIH work for you.*

So on October 11, 1988, more than 1,200 shouting ACT UP demonstrators descended on the FDA campus in Rockville, Maryland. During the nine-hour protest they demanded the FDA change its approval process to speed up release of new experimental drugs. They crawled onto the ledge above the building's main entrance and unfurled a SILENCE = DEATH banner and staged die-ins on the roads leading in and out of the campus. By the end of the day, 185 people had been arrested.

Did the protests work? Dr. Anthony Fauci of the National Institutes of Health later admitted to NBC News's *Dateline*, "After a little while, I began to get beyond the rhetoric and theater of the demonstrations and the smoke bombs, to really listen to what it is that they were saying, and it became clear to me, quite quickly, that most of what they said made absolute sense, was very logical and needed to be paid attention to."

ACT UP saw it a little differently. "It sort of felt like reaching the Wizard of Oz," said Mark Harrington, the group's science expert. "You got to the center of the whole system and there's just this schmuck behind the curtain. There was no guiding agenda, there was no leadership, there was no global strategy for how to deal with AIDS."

Fight AIDS!

A KEY member of Reagan's Presidential Commission on the HIV Epidemic was Cardinal John O'Connor, the archbishop of New York. In the eyes of ACT UP, he was also one of the worst members.

For years the LGBT community in New York City had been trying to get a human rights bill that outlawed discrimination based on sexual orientation through the city council. O'Connor and the archdiocese successfully blocked the effort for years, though it was finally approved in 1986. And even though Catholic hospitals were the largest health service providers in New York for those battling AIDS, they opposed any efforts to encourage condom use to fight the disease. The scene was set for a showdown.

On Sunday, December 10, 1989, about 4,500 protesters from ACT UP descended on St. Patrick's Cathedral in Manhattan. About 100 entered the church, where Cardinal O'Connor was saying mass. Many laid down in the center aisle and were dragged out by police. Others handcuffed themselves to pews. Activist Michael Petrelis stood up and shouted, "Stop killing us, Cardinal O'Connor!" to the horror of the parishioners. More than 100 people were arrested, 43 inside the cathedral.

Many later saw the "Stop the Church" protest as the beginning of the end for ACT UP—they had just gone too far. The group, however, was unapologetic. "As long as the epidemic rages and the Church fights in direct opposition to the policies recommended by responsible doctors, scientists, and public health officials, ACT UP will never be silent—not in the streets, not in the capital, and not even in the Church itself," it wrote in a press release.

Rude or not, it was hard to criticize ACT UP's list of successes. Through hundreds of loud, shaming protests, the group had forced the government and medical establishment into action. AIDS drugs were less expensive, new drugs were approved faster, and the government no longer ignored the crisis. "Surely ACT UP has taught everyone that you don't get anything by being nice, good little boys and girls," said Larry Kramer. "You do not get more with honey than vinegar."

And aside from ACT UP, the AIDS crisis had done something else: "Not only has the AIDS epidemic mobilized more gay men than

any other issue in the history of the gay movement," said historian Jeffrey Escoffier, "but it has led to a greatly increased appreciation of gay rights." More Americans were aware of the injustices suffered by the LGBT community as they sought treatment—restrictions in hospital visitations, health care, funeral arrangements, and inheritance rights. Nobody was talking much about same-sex marriage, hate crimes, and the right to serve openly in the military, but that too would change.

ACT UP protesters outside the FDA in Rockville, Maryland, October 11, 1988. ONE National Gay & Lesbian Archives, ACT UP/Los Angeles Papers

▲ ▼ ▲

"We're here, we're queer, get used to it!"

—Queer Nation chant

7

Setbacks and Victories

1990s

September 30, 1991 ▶ "Come out and face the people!" screamed the mob surrounding the Los Angeles County Art Museum. Inside, California governor Pete Wilson was attending a fundraiser. Just a day earlier, he had vetoed a bill—AB 101—which would have outlawed employment discrimination against the state's gays, lesbians, and bisexuals. During the previous year's election, Wilson said he would sign the bill. Now these citizens wanted him to explain himself.

Without speaking to the crowd, Wilson left in a motorcade for his suite at the Plaza Hotel. The protesters followed, and eventually clashed with police outside

◀ **ACT UP members stage a "lie-in" to protest at a fundraiser for Pete Wilson in Los Angeles, 1990.** ONE National Gay & Lesbian Archives, ACT UP/Los Angeles Papers

his hotel. Twelve were arrested before the night was over. The following day, Wilson addressed a ceremony at the 100th anniversary of Stanford University, where 300 activists near the stage tried to drown out his speech on "family values" by chanting "Shame! Shame! Shame!"

More rallies and demonstrations erupted across California. Seven thousand people marched on state office buildings in San Francisco, and a few smashed windows. Another confrontation took place outside the Ronald Reagan State Building in Los Angeles. Sacramento, San Diego, Garden Grove—protesters were everywhere, even lying on the runway to block flights at Los Angeles International Airport.

The uproar lasted 17 days. ACT UP's tactics had spread beyond AIDS issues.

▼ ▲ ▼

Queer Nation

IN THE late 1980s there was a disturbing increase in gay bashings—attacks on LGBT people by strangers and, sometimes, neighbors. There were more assaults reported in 1988 than in 1985, 1986, and 1987 combined. The LGBT community organized safety patrols, like the Pink Panthers, to protect those in larger cities, but the problem was far greater than something a few people could prevent.

Though the AIDS epidemic had brought out some of the best qualities of the LGBT community and its allies, it also brought out some of the worst among its critics and enemies. In 1988 the then-popular band Guns N' Roses released "One in a Million," a song that attacked gays, African Americans, and immigrants. And rap artists routinely badmouthed gays and lesbians with their lyrics.

So on March 20, 1990, about 60 activists gathered in New York to form a group to confront the growing homophobia. Many were from ACT UP. They eventually called themselves Queer Nation, an in-your-face name intended to "reclaim" a word that had so often been used to put them down. *Yeah, we're queer*, they were saying. *What's it to ya?*

The group started by holding what they called "Queer Nights Out." They would go to popular heterosexual bars to stage "kiss-ins" while chanting "We're here! We're queer! Get used to it!" They would also perform staged marriages in front of churches, pass out information on safe sex at suburban shopping malls, and confront politicians who were demonizing the LGBT community.

Queer Nation chapters soon popped up in fifty other cities. In Great Britain a similar group called OutRage! formed the same year.

And in 1992 a group called Lesbian Avengers was organized to specifically address women's issues and homophobia.

"The New Civil War"

AS USUALLY happens in the United States in the year leading up to a presidential election, certain issues divide the voting public. Politicians often exploit these issues to show the difference between themselves and their opponents. In the 1992 election, "family values" was one of the hot-button topics.

The term "family values" was used by conservatives, most of them Republicans, to criticize the growing visibility (and success) of the LGBT civil rights movement. Some felt so threatened they described the fight against gay rights as "The New Civil War."

Even slightly moderate politicians were not safe, like Republican president George H. W. Bush. There was never any doubt Bush would win his party's nomination. After all, he was the sitting president. But many in the party were angry that Bush had raised taxes and, in their view, hadn't spoken up enough on cultural issues such as opposition to gay rights. Conservative columnist Pat Buchanan decided to challenge him for the Republican nomination.

Buchanan got enough support during the primaries to demand an opening-night speech during the party's August convention. "There is a religious war going on in our country for the soul of America," he proclaimed at the event. "It is a cultural war, as critical to the kind of nation we will one day be as the Cold War itself." Delegates on the convention floor cheered and waved signs reading, FAMILY RIGHTS FOREVER, GAY RIGHTS NEVER. And on the same evening, just outside the convention hall, police on horseback charged after AIDS activists and Queer Nation protesters. Maybe Buchanan was right—it sort of looked like a civil war.

When Vice President Dan Quayle had a chance to speak, he claimed, "Americans try to raise their children to understand right and wrong, only to be told that every so-called 'lifestyle' is morally equivalent. That is wrong."

President Bush tried to soften the message on the convention's final night, but had already agreed to the campaign's "family values" theme. The phrase implied that those who disagreed with the Republicans' positions lacked families or values. Outside the bubble of the convention, however, the message struck many Americans as old fashioned at best, and cruel at worst.

Bush's Democratic opponent in the election, Bill Clinton, wasn't a perfect candidate for the LGBT community, either. As governor of Arkansas, Clinton had never been vocal on gay rights issues, and had even refused to meet with LGBT groups. But during the presidential campaign he promised to repeal the ban on openly gay and lesbian military servicemembers, and pledged more funding for AIDS research.

A month before the election, the full NAMES quilt was spread out on the National Mall surrounding the Washington Monument. It was a reminder to many of just how important it was to elect a supporter of the LGBT community.

On November 3, 1992, Bill Clinton was elected president. Three out of four gays and lesbians voted for him. But their celebration was short-lived—the same day, voters in Colorado handed the LGBT community its next challenge.

Amendment 2

IN 1992 a conservative group calling itself Colorado for Family Values (CFV) pushed a statewide vote on gay rights. Amendment 2, as it was known, would nullify—cancel—any existing gay rights measures in the state. At the time, only the cities of Denver, Boulder, and Aspen had such laws. The amendment would also prevent any local government from enacting a gay rights bill in the future.

CFV claimed that laws protecting gays and lesbians from discrimination were somehow giving them "special rights." In reality, gay rights measures like Denver voters had approved just two years earlier, granted no "special rights" to anyone. It simply said you could not fire anyone for being gay or lesbian, or kick them out of their apartment, or refuse to serve them at a restaurant. As a popular bumper sticker at the time stated: EQUAL RIGHTS ARE NOT SPECIAL RIGHTS.

Yet on election night, Colorado voters approved Amendment 2 by a 53–47 percent mar-

Many called for the boycott of Colorado after the 1992 election. Courtesy Center for the Study of Political Graphics

gin. There was an immediate call to boycott the state. Several national conventions canceled their plans to visit. However, nothing was as damaging to Colorado as the black eye it received from being labeled the "Hate State."

Before it went into effect, the law was challenged in court. Richard Evans, one of the governor's staff, and others, including tennis star Martina Navratilova, sued the state. And after moving through lower courts, on May 20, 1996, the US Supreme Court declared in a 6–3 ruling that Amendment 2 was unconstitutional because it forever shut the LGBT community out of the political process—the law prevented them from ever enacting a *new* law to overturn it.

The ruling in *Romer v. Evans* also threw out the "special rights" argument. It was one thing to make such a claim in a campaign, but it was tougher to support in a court of law. "We find nothing special in the protections Amendment 2 withholds. These are protections taken for granted by most people either because they already have them or do not need them," the majority wrote. "[Amendment 2] identifies persons by a single trait and then denies them protection across the board." That was clearly unconstitutional.

By the time the decision was handed down, many Colorado citizens were thrilled to see the whole embarrassing episode just go away.

Don't Ask, Don't Tell

SHORTLY AFTER he was sworn in as president, Bill Clinton announced that he intended to sign an executive order ending the ban on

ACTIVITY
BOYCOTT

FOR CENTURIES, citizens have used boycotts to force change. American colonists boycotted British tea imports to protest unfair taxes, a campaign that led to the Boston Tea Party. The 1955–56 Montgomery Bus Boycott brought an end to segregated seating on city buses. And people, organizations, and countries boycotted South Africa from the 1960s to the 1980s to bring an end to apartheid.

You may not know it, but the adults in your life have probably been involved in a boycott at some time. They may still be boycotting. Find out! Interview several adults, and ask them the following questions:

1. Is there any product you have boycotted by choosing not to buy it? Why?

2. Is there a store where you refuse to shop, or restaurant where you won't eat? Is this because of an organized campaign or just your own personal boycott?

3. Have you ever been part of an organized boycott, such as a letter writing campaign or a protest march?

4. Did the boycott come to an end? Why?

If the adult's boycott was part of an organized campaign, go online with the adult's help and research it. Did it work? Did it fail? Is it still going on?

open gay and lesbian service in the US military. He thought it could be done easily, "with the stroke of a pen," and many in the LGBT community believed it as well. They didn't take into account, however, how Washington really worked, or didn't.

LGBT veterans led the March on Washington for Lesbian, Gay, and Bi Equal Rights & Liberation, April 25, 1993. Photo by author

There was an immediate uproar from most of the Republicans in Congress, and a good number of Democrats, as well as the military establishment. Almost immediately, Clinton said he would delay the decision for six months.

On April 25, 1993, more than 800,000 LGBT marchers and allies descended on the nation's capital for the March on Washington for Lesbian, Gay, and Bi Equal Rights & Liberation. The rally had been planned for years, so it was not a response to the gays-in-the-military issue. However, that issue took center stage anyway.

President Clinton met with LGBT leaders in the Oval Office on April 16, a week before the march, but left town during the event. The parade, led by LGBT veterans, stepped off at noon and continued for seven hours, breaking the record for the largest protest in DC history.

The march meant less, however, than a three-man "fact-finding tour" conducted by Senator Sam Nunn, Senator John Warner, and General Colin Powell, Chairman of the Joint Chiefs of Staff. In May 1993 they toured the USS *Baton Rouge* submarine to ask sailors their thoughts about the proposed change that would end the ban on openly gay service members.

Conservative Republican leader Barry Goldwater surprised many when he criticized the ban, saying, "You don't need to be 'straight' to fight and die for your country. You just need to shoot straight." But it was too little, too late.

Calls to the White House ran more than 10-to-1 against the change. Nunn, Powell, and Defense Secretary Les Aspin worked out a deal called "Don't Ask, Don't Tell." Servicemembers would not be asked their sexual orientation, but they were not allowed to speak about it, either. And if they were found out to be gay or lesbian, they could still be thrown out of the service.

The new policy pleased almost nobody, particularly the LGBT community. President Clinton appeared tone-deaf to the claim that he might have made things *worse*. "When a president takes on tough issues, takes tough stands, tries to get things done in a democracy, he may not get one hundred percent. Was I wrong to get eighty-five?"

Perhaps yes. To seal the deal, instead of being a guideline for the military to follow, the US Congress made the new policy a *law*. This made it impossible for any future president to change anything without the approval of the House and Senate. In other words, Don't Ask, Don't Tell would be military policy for many, many years to come.

Interestingly, the US military often worked side-by-side with allies, such as the European members of NATO, the North Atlantic Treaty Organization. Most of them already allowed gay and lesbian service members who worked alongside American troops.

International Developments

THOUGH TREMENDOUS progress had been made in the United States during the 1970s, setbacks in the conservative 1980s and the AIDS crisis allowed LGBT civil rights in other countries to advance beyond America's.

In 1989, Denmark became the first country to legalize same-sex unions. Because of objections from religious groups, they were called "registered partnerships" rather than marriages. (Norway followed, granting registered partnerships in 1993, and Sweden did the same in 1995.) On October 1, 1989, Danish gay rights pioneers Axel and Eigil Axgil became the first couple united under the law. The pair had been together for 32 years, and had already taken the same last name.

In 1994 South Africa, newly freed from decades of oppression under apartheid, became the first country in the world to enshrine equal protection for gays and lesbians into its constitution. South Africans had Simon Nkoli, head of the Gay and Lesbian Organization of Witwatersrand (GLOW), to thank for it. Nkoli and GLOW had joined the fight to end apartheid, which landed him in prison for four years. After being freed, he met with South African president Nelson Mandela and other leaders, like Patrick Lekota of the African National Congress.

Sir Ian McKellen (1939–)

Known to millions of moviegoers as Gandalf the Grey from the *Lord of the Rings* films, actor Ian McKellen came out in 1988 to protest the British government's infamous Section 28 of the Local Government Act. The law made it illegal for a teacher or government official to "promote homosexuality or... promote the teaching in any maintained school of the acceptability of homosexuality as a pretended family relationship."

When it was announced by the government of conservative Prime Minister Margaret Thatcher, Section 28 sparked the largest LGBT protest ever seen in London. During the debate over the bill in the House of Lords, a group of lesbians dropped rope ladders over the balcony railing and descended into the chamber to disrupt the discussion. Protesters also interrupted a live broadcast of the BBC's *Six O'Clock News* to make a direct appeal to television viewers. The bill passed anyway. (Section 28 was not repealed until 2003.)

© Mary McCartney

At the time, McKellen cofounded Stonewall, England's main gay rights organization. "It was wrongly assumed that I wished to become some sort of leader among gay activists," McKellen later said. "Whereas in reality I was happier to be a foot soldier." But whether he wanted it or not, McKellen became a leader of the LGBT community in Great Britain. Because of this, some objected when he was knighted in 1991, becoming the first openly gay man to receive the honor.

"How could we say that men and women like Simon, who had put their shoulders to the wheel to end apartheid, how could we say that they should now be discriminated against?" wondered Lekota. They couldn't.

Years later, Nobel Peace Prize winner Archbishop Desmond Tutu predicted, "I have no doubt that in the future, the laws that criminalize so many forms of love and human commitment will look the way the apartheid laws do to us now—so obviously wrong."

Classroom Uproar

ONE OF the things that sparked the antigay backlash in England was a children's book, *Jenny Lives with Eric and Martin* by Susanne Bösche. It had been purchased with taxpayer money by several school libraries in London, and some of those taxpayers were angry. Of course, plenty of other taxpayers were LGBT. Didn't they have a right to see their lives reflected in the local library?

A similar controversy erupted in New York City in 1992. That year the city's public schools adopted a multicultural curriculum called "Children of the Rainbow." And though the word "rainbow" made some people think "gay," only two sentences in the 443-page document even *mentioned* LGBT issues: "Be aware of the changing concept of *family* in today's society," and, "Educators have the potential to help increase the tolerance and acceptance of the lesbian/gay community and to decrease the staggering number of hate crimes perpetrated against them."

There were also three LGBT children's books—*Heather Has Two Mommies*, *Daddy's Roommate*, and *Gloria Goes to Gay Pride*—listed among hundreds of other multicultural titles in its bibliography. That's it!

Nevertheless, one local school board, District 24 in Queens, refused to approve the curriculum. "We will not accept two people of the same sex engaged in deviant sex practices as a 'family,'" pronounced Mary Cummins, the board president. She also accused Joseph Fernandez, chancellor of the New York City Public Schools, of perpetrating "as big a lie as any concocted by Hitler or Stalin." Was she serious?

Heather Has Two Mommies seemed to ignite most of the anger, not only for its lesbian characters, but because it discussed divorce . . . something children were quite familiar with. Author Lesléa Newman had written the picture book after a lesbian friend complained, "We have no books to read our daughter that show our type of family. Somebody should write one." So Newman did.

For failing to approve the curriculum, Chancellor Fernandez suspended the entire District 24 board. The city's main school board then un-suspended them and (eventually) forced Fernandez out of his job instead.

AIDS in the '90s

OF COURSE, the AIDS virus continued on its destructive path. By the summer of 1989, the number of AIDS cases reported in the United States passed 100,000, and 59,000 of those infected had already died.

And yet, something *had* changed. In 1989, ACT UP leaders were asked to speak at the Sixth Annual AIDS Conference in San Francisco, and they got a standing ovation. The group's aggressive, educated, and honest approach to the crisis had finally gained the respect of the medical establishment. In 1990 Dr. Anthony Fauci invited five members of ACT UP to his office at the NIH, then put them on the AIDS Clinical Trials Group Committee. And even more patients willingly volunteered to be subjects in medical studies for new, experimental treatments.

In late 1993, Hollywood released *Philadelphia*, the first mainstream film about the AIDS crisis, starring Tom Hanks and Denzel Washington. When Hanks won an Oscar for Best Actor, he made a plea for tolerance:

I would not be standing here if it weren't for two very important men in my life. . . .

ACTIVITY

READ A BANNED BOOK

EACH SEPTEMBER the American Library Association (ALA) brings attention to the issue of library censorship through Banned Books Week. Since it first began in 1982, the ALA has documented more than 11,000 challenges to books nationwide. Many of these books deal with LGBT subjects, most recently *And Tango Makes Three*, *The Perks of Being a Wallflower*, and *Uncle Bobby's Wedding*.

Contact your local library and see what they are doing for Banned Books Week, and visit during September. Often libraries have displays of banned books, or have programs about intellectual freedom. You can also find lists of books that have been banned or challenged at www.ala.org/bbooks/frequentlychallengedbooks. Have you read any of them?

*Mr. Rawley Farnsworth, who was my high
school drama teacher, . . . and one of my
classmates, . . . Mr. John Gilkerson. I mention
their names because they are two of the finest
gay Americans, two wonderful men that I
had the good fortune to be associated with, to
fall under their inspiration at such a young
age. I wish my babies could have the same
sort of teacher, the same sort of friends.*

AIDS was also part of the third season of
MTV's *The Real World*, which started in June
1994. One of its cast members, Pedro Zamora,
was HIV positive. It was the first chance for
many viewers to see people living side-by-side
with a person with AIDS. Zamora later exchanged vows with his partner, Sean Sasser, before dying in Miami on November 11, 1994, one
day after the final episode aired. He was only 22.

And then, in 1996, a breakthrough! Researchers came up with a three-drug combination—
"the AIDS cocktail"—that for many patients
appeared to halt the virus's destructive progress. And not just that, it *reversed* many of the
worst symptoms of AIDS. People who were
bedridden were able to get up and walk again,
and gain weight. Some called the AIDS cocktail the Lazarus drug after the biblical story of
a man who rose from the dead.

Of course, the three-drug combination was
not a cure for AIDS, but for the first time those
who were HIV positive could manage their disease, like people with diabetes do. That was a
tremendous step forward.

Two years later, readers of the *Bay Area
Reporter* picked up the August 13, 1998, issue
to see the blaring headline: No Obits. For 17
years, the LGBT paper in the San Francisco
Bay Area ran obituary notices—obits—submitted by friends or family members to mark
the passing of people who had died of AIDS.
Sometimes there were pages filled with obitu-
aries. But for the first two weeks in August
1998, the paper hadn't received any notices,
and the deadline loomed. "It was like watching a no-hitter in baseball unfolding," said
Mike Salinas, the news editor. "We didn't really want to discuss it until it became obvi-
ous that it was going to happen. We held our
breath waiting."

The LGBT community had lost so much, and
so many. Yet it persevered, and brought people
closer together than they ever had been before.
Vito Russo, for one, knew the day would come,
and he told a crowd of protesters outside the
New York State Assembly in May 1988:

*Someday the AIDS crisis will be over. . . .
And when that day comes, when that day has
come and gone, there will be a people alive on
this earth—gay people and straight people,
black people and white people, men and*

women—who will hear the story that once there was a terrible disease in this country, and all over the world, and that a brave group of people stood up and fought, and in some cases gave their lives, so that other people might live and be free.

Russo did not survive to tell that story. The man who forever changed the way people looked at movies, who helped found the GAA and ACT UP, died of AIDS-related complications in November 1990.

But others did make it. Guy Clark, who ran a flower stand in San Francisco's Castro, reflected on the community's unexpected victories. "This tragedy—it taught us how to be humble. It taught us how to be honest. It taught us how to love in spite of what's at the end of the tunnel."

Building Gay-Straight Alliances

IN THE fall of 1995 Kelli Peterson, a senior at East High School in Salt Lake City, turned in her paperwork for a new afterschool club: the Gay-Straight Alliance (GSA). As clubs went, it was small—just 15 students. Most were LGBT, but a few were friends or family members. GSAs already existed elsewhere. Every high school in Massachusetts had one. Still, some

ACTIVITY

TRY A DAY WITH(OUT) ART

WHEN THE ORGANIZATION Visual AIDS began "A Day Without Art" in 1989, it was intended as a day of mourning and remembrance for all artists lost to AIDS. Some museums and galleries closed so that their staff could volunteer with AIDS charities in their communities. Others removed famous works of art or showcased works about AIDS. It was a reminder to patrons of the impact of AIDS on the artistic community.

In 1996 the annual event was changed to A Day With(out) Art. Now on December 1, instead of closing for the day, the same museums and galleries highlight artists dealing with HIV/AIDS, both in their lives and in their work.

A Day With(out) Art is held on December 1 each year, which is also World AIDS Day. Call your local art museum or gallery to see if they are doing anything for the day. If you can attend their events, do.

at the Utah school didn't like the idea of a gay youth group and wanted to stop it.

Back in 1984, the US Congress passed the Equal Access Act. It mandated that if a public school allowed *any* extracurricular clubs, it had to allow *all* clubs. That included Bible study clubs, which was the real reason the law was passed—some schools were worried that Bible study clubs violated the separation of church and state, and would not allow them to meet on school grounds. This law prevented schools from doing that.

Peterson didn't know about the law when she proposed the club, but she soon learned that the law also applied to her club. She reminded the school board that the law protected the GSA when she addressed a public hearing about it.

The basis of this club is to end hate, intolerance, ignorance, and fear. This group was formed by students, is led by students, and is attended by students. The law is very clear regarding the rights of clubs. Gay and bisexual students have the same inalienable rights as heterosexual students have. This is not a religious issue or a moral issue, this is a legal issue, and the law is very clear. So I encourage this board not to break the law. I believe the students have behaved responsibly. I hope you do, too.

The board had two options: allow the GSA to meet (and require students to get parental permission to join), or cancel all extracurricular clubs. They voted for the second option. Just days later, the state legislature passed a law banning the use of public facilities for any organization dealing with human sexuality, criminal activity, or bigotry.

But Peterson wasn't giving up that easily. She and her friends organized a student walkout at East High, not just by members of the GSA, but all students who had been affected by the club cancellations. The walk-out spread to other schools in Salt Lake City, and soon thousands of teens were marching on the state capitol building.

The protests and negative attention got the legislature to repeal its law, but the school board continued to ban extracurricular clubs. Sort of. In the 1997–98 school year, it allowed the Future Homemakers of America to meet, putting the school in violation of the Equal Access Act. The GSA sued and won, and in the fall of 2000, East High finally allowed the Gay-Straight Alliance to meet. The club still meets to this day.

The So-Called Defense of Marriage Act

LIKE ALL gay and lesbian couples in the 1980s, Ninia Baehr and Genora Dancel could not buy joint health insurance or name each other on life insurance policies. As far as their home state of Hawaii was concerned, under the law they were strangers. They weren't blood relatives. They weren't married. And if the state didn't recognize them as a couple, why should an insurance company?

But maybe that could change. On December 17, 1990, Baehr and Dancel asked for a wedding license at the Department of Health's vital records office in Honolulu. They were denied. Two other same-sex couples were turned away that same day. In May 1991 they all filed a discrimination suit against the state. And four months later, a judge dismissed their claim.

The case, known as *Baehr v. Lewin*, was appealed to the Hawaii Supreme Court. In May 1993 that court ruled that the couples could sue claiming sex discrimination. When Hawaii became a state in 1959, its constitution specifically outlawed discrimination based upon sex. In other words, what right did Hawaii have to deny a person the right to marry another, based only on that other person's sex? The court ordered a retrial.

Across the nation, opponents of same-sex marriage freaked out. If the Hawaii court ruled that gays and lesbians could get married—and it looked like a possibility—could the same thing happen in other states? Or if a same-sex couple visiting Hawaii got married, could they force their home state to recognize the marriage? (That was already true for opposite-sex marriages.)

Social conservatives mobilized. In early 1996 they held a "Campaign to Protect Marriage" rally in Iowa on the eve of that state's presidential caucuses. Every Republican candidate pledged to support their efforts, including the eventual nominee, Senator Bob Dole. Donald Kaul, a columnist for the *Des Moines Register*, saw through the stunt: "Bad enough that they had the rally at all," Kaul wrote, "but to see the men who would be president come one-by-one to suck up to the hateful demagogues who make up the leadership of the 'pro-family' movement was revolting."

In Washington, Congress began debating a bill called the Defense of Marriage Act—DOMA. The bill would prevent any legally married same-sex couple from receiving *any* of the 1,138 federal benefits given to married couples—the right to file joint tax returns, receive Social Security survival benefits if a partner died, spousal inheritance, and joint parenting, to say nothing of the benefits that extended to their children. It also nullified (made invalid) the "full faith and credit" clause of the US Constitution for same-sex marriage. No state would be required to honor a gay marriage performed in another state.

The debate was swift and often mean-spirited. But there were bright spots too. Rep. Nancy Pelosi dragged out a large photo of Del Martin and Phyllis Lyon, who lived in her San Francisco district. "Their commitment, their love, and their happiness are a source of strength to all who know them," she told her colleagues gathered in the House. "Their relationship is not a threat to *anyone's* marriage."

DOMA passed the House by a whopping 342 to 67 margin. It passed the Senate by an even larger percentage—85 to 14. Many in the LGBT community saw the bill as an effort to embarrass President Clinton on the eve of the 1996 election, and to drive a wedge between the president and his LGBT supporters. It succeeded in doing both.

Clinton signed the law in the middle of the night, but later bragged about it in Christian radio commercials and campaign literature used in the South. Gay and lesbian voters were furious.

Meanwhile, state legislatures were passing their own versions of DOMA. Before the end of 1996, sixteen states had enacted bans on same-sex marriage.

After a three-year delay in the Hawaii trial, and after DOMA had become law and Bill Clinton was reelected, Judge Kevin Chang finally ruled on December 3, 1996, that same-sex couples could marry in the state. He also put a hold on the decision . . . the state supreme court would still have to hear another appeal.

While waiting on the high court, the Hawaii legislature passed a Reciprocal Beneficiaries Law in 1997 to grant some legal protections to gay and lesbian couples—hospital visitation, joint ownership of property, inheritance, and more. It was the first of its kind in the nation.

A year later, Hawaii voters approved a constitutional ban on same-sex marriage by 69 to 29 percent. Then finally, in December 1999, the state supreme court ruled the *Baehr v. Lewin* case moot—no longer worth discussing. Voters had "resolved" the issue while the state courts dragged their feet for ten years.

As bad as it seemed to the LGBT community at the time, hidden in the dark cloud of the same-sex marriage debate was a silver lining of increased understanding and acceptance. For many Americans, this was the first time they saw gay and lesbian couples even *ask* for marriage rights. In 1988, only 12 percent of Americans supported same-sex marriage, but by 1996, the year DOMA passed, 27 percent did. Attitudes were changing.

Even better, the fight for marriage had gained supporters in the LGBT community. Evan Wolfson, who had served as one of the lawyers on the Hawaii case, launched the Marriage Project at Lambda Legal, the nation's first legal organization dedicated to achieving full equality for LGBT people.

Coming Out Everywhere

IN THE 1990s, there was an explosion of LGBT organizations as more people became comfortable being out. Though some groups had started years earlier, the decade saw new LGBT organizations formed around racial and ethnic diversity, disabilities, religious affiliations, sports teams, hobby clubs, and more.

Little by little, gay and lesbian characters started showing up on network television shows as well. In the 1970s and '80s, if they appeared at all, they were often stereotypes. But as more viewers knew LGBT family and friends, the characters had to be more realistic. They had jobs, partners, *lives*, and didn't just show up as the butt of a joke.

In 1992 the daytime soap opera *One Life to Live* introduced a new character, gay teen Billy Douglas, played by Ryan Phillippe. Some warned the 17-year-old actor that the role would hurt his career, but he was glad he did it. "I felt lucky to play the first gay teenager on television not just daytime but television, period. What was so amazing... was the response I got through fan letters that my mother and I would read together," recalled Phillippe. "Kids who'd never seen themselves represented on TV or in movies would write to say what a huge support they found it to be."

Yet the biggest event in LGBT television history was still to come. In 1997, Ellen DeGeneres, star of the hit sitcom *Ellen*, came out of the closet. The headline over her smiling face on the cover of *Time* magazine confirmed, "Yep,

I'm Gay." The admission caused less commotion than the announcement that her on-screen character, Ellen Morgan, would be coming out as well.

But first they had to film it, and the hate mail rolled in. On the day the scene was filmed, the studio got a bomb threat. Chrysler announced that it would not advertise during the episode, and Wendy's dropped its sponsorship of the show altogether. The ABC affiliate in Birmingham, Alabama, refused to air it.

One in five Americans tuned in to watch Ellen Morgan (left, played by Ellen DeGeneres) come out on April 30, 1997. ABC/Photofest, © ABC

DeGeneres didn't back down, and on April 30, 1997, an estimated 42 million viewers tuned in. As the season went on, ABC began each episode with a warning: Caution: This show contains adult content. "Adult content?" DeGeneres later fumed. "You turn on any other show on television and they're sleeping with each other and they're not married and that's OK for kids to see. You can see people killing each other. There was none of that on my show, but you can't see two women holding hands or saying, 'I love you.'"

After struggling for another season, *Ellen* was canceled. Still, DeGeneres was proud of what she'd done. "It didn't matter if I was going to lose all of my money or my career," she said. "It was what I had to do."

In the end, she didn't lose either. DeGeneres would go on to provide the voice for Dory in *Finding Nemo* (and later, *Finding Dory*), and in 2003 launched a popular daytime talk show. In 2012 she received the nation's highest honor for comedy, the Mark Twain Prize for American Humor.

Hate Crimes Become National Stories

Around 5 o'clock in the evening of October 7, 1998, Aaron Kreifels was riding his bike along Snowy Mountain View Road on the outskirts of Laramie, Wyoming, when he spotted what he thought was a scarecrow tied to a fence. Looking closer, he realized it was the body of an unconscious young man, his face coated in blood. *God, the kid's been crucified*, thought Kreifels.

Paramedics rushed the victim, Matthew Shepard, to the hospital, and the police soon had two suspects in custody. Shepard had left the Fireside Bar on the morning of the 7th with two strangers, Aaron McKinney and Russell Henderson, but instead of giving him a ride home they beat him, robbed him, and left him to die.

Five days later, Shepard passed away in a Colorado hospital, his parents by his bedside. "Go home, give your kids a hug, and don't let a day go by without telling them that you love them," Judy Shepard, Matthew's mother, said in a statement.

The story was front-page news by the time Shepard's memorial service was held in Casper. The Rev. Fred Phelps of the antigay Westboro Baptist Church showed up to celebrate the 21-year-old's death. Phelps and his followers had taunted the LGBT community for years, but it was the first time most Americans saw them in action. Hundreds of mourners sang "Amazing Grace" outside St. Mark's Episcopal Church, trying to drown out the twelve protesters, but they could not obscure their hand-held signs—MATT IN HELL, AIDS CURES FAGS, and NO SPECIAL LAWS FOR FAGS.

When Henderson and McKinney went on trial in the spring, Phelps returned. By that time Romaine Patterson, a lesbian friend of Shepard's, had come up with a plan. She and her friends dressed as "Angels of Peace" with enormous, tall wings. "The idea was to keep Phelps from being on television," Patterson said, "and we also didn't want Matthew's parents to see these guys." Standing shoulder-to-shoulder, they could block Phelps from view.

"Phelps had arrived [at the courthouse] about ten minutes before we did. . . . He was yelling and they were all shaking their signs in the air. So we get there and the looks on people's faces were amazing. . . . Fred Phelps and the rest of them just shut up and didn't say a word."

Before the trial began, Russell Henderson, a former Eagle Scout, pled guilty to kidnapping, robbery, and felony murder, and drew two life sentences without parole. Aaron McKinney hoped to use a "gay panic defense," claiming that Shepard had tried to touch him, but the judge wouldn't allow it. McKinney was eventually found guilty of felony murder. With this conviction, he faced the death sentence, but was spared by Shepard's parents.

"I would like nothing better than to see you die, Mr. McKinney," said Dennis Shepard at the sentencing hearing. "However, this is the time to begin the healing process. To show mercy to someone who refused to show any mercy. . . . May you have a long life, and may you thank Matthew every day for it."

The murder of Matthew Shepard finally personalized for many Americans the issue of violence against LGBT citizens. There were soon more reminders.

On July 5, 1999, Pvt. Calvin Glover beat Pvt. Barry Winchell with a baseball bat while he was sleeping in the barracks at Fort Campbell, Kentucky. Winchell died the next day. The US Army tried to cover it up by calling it an "altercation between soldiers." But investigators from the Servicemembers Legal Defense Net-

The Angels of Peace outside the Albany County Courthouse in Laramie, Wyoming, 1999.

© Adam Mastoon/Corbis

work (SLDN) discovered that Winchell was targeted for dating a transgender woman.

The same year, Hollywood released *Boys Don't Cry*, based on the 1993 murder of Brandon Teena in Falls City, Nebraska. Named Teena Brandon at birth, the 21-year-old was killed by two young men when they discovered he was transgender. (Two witnesses were killed at the same time.) Hillary Swank played Teena in the film, and won an Academy Award for Best Actress. She ended her acceptance speech by saying,

> *I want to thank Brandon Teena for being such an inspiration to us all. His legacy lives on through our movie to remind us to always be ourselves, to follow our hearts, to not conform. I pray for the day when we not only accept our differences, but we actually celebrate our diversity.*

In the wake of these cases, there was a new push for a Federal Hate Crimes Act, led by Matthew Shepard's parents. "I can't bring [Matthew] back," said Dennis Shepard, "but I can do my best to see that this never, ever happens to another person or another family again." The bill stalled in Congress, however, because of lobbying by Focus on the Family, the Family Research Council, and other religious organizations. Focus on the Family claimed the bill was "a hate crime against parents" who wanted to teach their children that homosexuality is a sin. It didn't matter that, according to the Southern Poverty Law Center, more than half

PERFORM A MONOLOGUE FROM *THE LARAMIE PROJECT*

FOUR WEEKS after Matthew Shepard's murder, Moisés Kaufman and nine members of the Tectonic Theater Project traveled to Laramie to interview those closest to the case. Over the next year and a half they gathered more than 200 interviews with everyone from Matthew's parents to Rev. Phelps. The interviews were later compiled into a powerful play, *The Laramie Project*. In it, the people of Laramie speak for themselves about the tragedy and how it affected their lives.

The play is still popular with high school, college, and local theater groups. You might even be able to see it by checking out the play's community website, http://community.laramie project.org, which lists upcoming performances nationwide.

If you can't attend a performance, put together a recital of your own. Find a copy of the play at your local library, then select a character that you find interesting. Can you memorize and perform a monologue from the play? Or, with friends, select a scene that you can act out together.

of reported physical hate crimes in 1994 were against the LGBT community.

Trouble in the Boy Scouts

JAMES DALE loved the Boy Scouts. He started as a Cub Scout when he was eight years old, and eventually earned his Eagle Scout badge. "Boy Scouts was community. It was a place where I felt I belonged," he said. "In the Boy Scouts, I could be who I was. They valued me for who I was."

Or so he thought. In college he volunteered as an assistant scoutmaster, Troop 73, but in 1990 was expelled from the organization. Why? Not because he had done anything wrong; the Boy Scouts discovered that Dale was also the head of the Lesbian/Gay Alliance at Rutgers University. The organization claimed that Dale had violated the Boy Scout Oath to be "morally straight." Just *being* gay was enough. He disagreed, and took the Boy Scouts to court.

In 1999 the New Jersey Supreme Court unanimously ruled that the Boy Scouts of New Jersey had discriminated against Dale, but it was overruled by the US Supreme Court a year later. In a 5–4 decision, the high court claimed that as an "expressive association"—one that promotes a certain viewpoint—the Boy Scouts could ignore the antidiscrimination laws of the state.

The four justices who dissented had a different opinion. Justice John Paul Stevens wrote, "The only apparent explanation, then, for the majority's holding... is that homosexuals are simply so different from the rest of society that their presence alone—unlike other individual's—should be singled out for special 1st Amendment treatment."

The ruling in *Boy Scouts of America v. Dale* was a reminder to the LGBT community that even though it had made tremendous progress in the previous decades, there was still a long way to go. As far as the law was concerned, they were still second-class citizens—prevented from marrying, barred from military service, and open to discrimination in their jobs and where they chose to live.

Much of that would soon change.

▲ ▼ ▲

"Indeed, Miss Manners has come to believe that the basic political division in this country is not between liberals and conservatives but between those who believe that they should have a say in the love lives of strangers and those who do not."

—Judith Martin, better known as columnist "Miss Manners"

8

Things Get Better

2000-Present

September 11, 2001 ▶ In the chaos at the World Trade Center on the morning of September 11, 2001, Father Mychal Judge, a chaplain with the New York City fire department, knelt over the body of firefighter Daniel Suhr to administer the Last Rites. Moments later, in the lobby of the North Tower, Father Mike was struck and killed by debris from the collapse of the South Tower.

Meanwhile, in the skies over Pennsylvania, a group of passengers on United Airlines Flight 93 decided to rush the cockpit of their hijacked airplane. One of those passengers was Mark Bingham, a public relations executive and six-foot-four-inch, 225-pound player on the San Francisco Fog Rugby Football Club. Bingham and the other passengers broke through the door, fought with the hijackers, and crashed the plane in a field near Shanksville, preventing it from reaching its intended target. All aboard died.

◀ **Two newlyweds outside San Francisco city hall, February 16, 2004.** Photo by Daniel Nicoletta

Back in New York, firefighters brought Father Mike's dust-covered body to St. Peter's Catholic Church and laid it in front of the altar. Later it was taken to the Engine 1/Ladder 24 firehouse. The coroner listed Mychal Judge as Victim 00001 of the World Trade Center attacks.

Two days later, from the safety of their Virginia television studios, Jerry Falwell and Pat Robertson discussed the terrorist attacks via satellite on *The 700 Club*. "I really believe that the pagans, and the abortionists, and the feminists, and the gays and the lesbians . . . all of them who have tried to secularize America—I point the finger in their face and say, 'You helped this happen,'" Falwell proclaimed. "Well, I totally concur," Robertson chimed in.

Most of the fire crews in New York didn't know Judge was gay, and didn't care once they learned. Father Mike had been a chaplain in the department since 1992, but he also ministered to the homeless and to a chapter of DignityUSA, a community of LGBT Catholics. Mark Bingham was also gay, as were many of that day's victims, including police officers and firefighters.

Falwell and Robertson were widely criticized, and looked even worse as more became known about that day's heroes. In June 2002 the US Congress voted on the Mychal Judge Act, to provide federal death benefits to same-sex partners of public safety officers killed in the line of duty. It was opposed by Focus on the Family and the Traditional Values Coalition. It passed anyway.

Father Mike's helmet was later presented to Pope John Paul II.

▼ ▲ ▼

Civil Unions in Vermont

JOHN CUSHING, the town clerk in Milton, Vermont, was kind but clear—he could not give Lois Farnham and Holly Puterbaugh a marriage license. It was against state law.

The couple wasn't surprised or angry. Cushing was a friend, and they'd called him the day before to let him know they would be coming by. And though deep down they wanted a marriage license, that day they were happy to get a letter from Cushing refusing their application.

In order to file a civil rights lawsuit, a person must first have proof that he or she has been treated unfairly. Now they had it. Two other couples, Nina Beck and Stacy Jolles, and Stan Baker and Peter Harrington, got similar letters that same day. All had been carefully selected by lawyers from the Vermont Freedom to Marry Task Force.

On July 22, 1997, these couples filed a lawsuit saying they had been unfairly denied the right to marry. The *Baker* case, as it became known, took two and a half years to make it to the Vermont Supreme Court. Finally, on December 20, 1999, the judges handed down a unanimous decision: the couples had been discriminated against. To fix the situation, the state legislature was ordered to extend to gay and lesbian couples wanting to marry all the civil rights given to married heterosexual couples. The decision said to call it marriage or call it something else, but if lawmakers didn't act the court would come up with a plan of its own.

After much public debate, the legislature settled on a compromise that pleased neither side, but was a step forward. Same-sex couples could receive a "civil union" with many of the legal benefits of a heterosexual marriage, but it wouldn't be called a "marriage."

The law went into effect July 1, 2000. Just after midnight Carolyn Conrad and Kathleen Peterson became the first same-sex couple in Vermont to be granted a civil union. After signing their license in the Brattleboro town clerk's office, they walked across the street to the public park and had a ceremony. Puterbaugh and Farnham got their license at 9 o'clock that morning, followed by a religious ceremony at the First Congregational Church in Burlington.

The Vermont civil unions case was the LGBT community's first big win on marriage. Over the next 15 years, it would be repeated over and over and over again.

Big Legal Victories

IN 2003, two courts issued rulings that would forever change the course of LGBT civil rights in the United States.

The first case, *Lawrence v. Texas*, was handed down by the US Supreme Court on June 26, 2003. Five years earlier, police in Houston, Texas, had entered the apartment of John Lawrence and found him in bed with Tyron Garner. The men were arrested under the state's Homosexual Conduct Law that made it illegal for gay men to have sex.

After a night in jail, Lawrence and Garner decided to fight the charges. The government didn't have the right to harass gay people in their own homes, the men believed. They pled "no contest" to the charges, paid the $125 fines, and then sued.

The case was eventually heard by the highest court in the land. The lawyer for Texas argued that the state had the right "to prohibit certain immoral conduct"—the Supreme Court's ruling in *Bowers v. Hardwick* (page 107) said it could. The lawyers for Lawrence and Garner argued that the law singled out gays and lesbians for persecution.

The Supreme Court rarely admits that it made a mistake, but writing for the 6–3 majority, Justice Anthony Kennedy did just that. "*Bowers* was not correct when it was decided, and it is not correct today," he wrote. "The petitioners are entitled to respect for their private lives. The state cannot demean their existence or control their destiny by making their private sexual conduct a crime."

Justice Antonin Scalia not only disagreed, he flipped out. "Many Americans do not want persons who openly engage in homosexual conduct as partners in their business, as scoutmasters for their children, as teachers in their children's schools, or as boarders in their home," he wrote in his dissent, and accused the other justices of having "largely signed on to the so-called homosexual agenda." He warned that the ruling could open the floodgates for LGBT civil rights. On that, he was absolutely correct.

It didn't take long, because another marriage equality case was moving through the Massachusetts courts. Briefly mentioning the *Lawrence v. Texas* decision, saying that it supported "the core concept of common human dignity," the Massachusetts Supreme Judicial Court ruled on November 18 that gay and lesbian couples should have the right to marry.

Writing for the 4–3 majority in *Goodridge v. Department of Health*, Chief Justice Margaret Marshall stated, "The Massachusetts Constitution affirms the dignity and equality of all individuals. It forbids the creation of second-class citizens. . . . [The Commonwealth] has failed to identify any constitutionally adequate reason for denying civil marriage to same-sex couples."

The judges also said that civil unions were not enough—same-sex couples had to be of-

Julie (left) and Hillary Goodridge, who brought the Massachusetts lawsuit, finally received a marriage license on May 17, 2004. Between them is their daughter, Annie. © Jessica Rinaldi/Reuters/Corbis

fered *marriage*. The court then ordered the legislature to craft a plan in 180 days, which it did. Both Governor Mitt Romney and the Catholic Church fought it every step of the way. Romney even went so far as to bring up a 1913 law against miscegenation—interracial marriage—to bar non-residents from coming to Massachusetts to wed. Nothing worked.

Just after midnight on May 17, 2004, on the 50th anniversary of the decision in *Brown v. Board of Education*, 752 same-sex couples marched into city halls across Massachusetts and tied the knot. Some even quoted from the *Goodridge* court decision during their vows.

Outside Cambridge city hall, crowds sang "America the Beautiful" and "This Land Is Your Land." When the Rev. Fred Phelps and his followers showed up with their hate-covered signs, as they had so many times before, the crowd cheered. And they had their own signs: You're Not in Kansas Anymore and See, Chicken Little, the Sky Is Not Falling.

Phelps left 15 minutes later.

The Winter of Love

San Francisco mayor Gavin Newsom sat in the gallery of the US House of Representatives, listening to President Bush's 2004 State of the Union address. He had been invited by House Minority Leader Nancy Pelosi, whose dis-

Perez v. Sharp and *Loving v. Virginia*

THE LEGAL GROUNDWORK FOR SAME-SEX MARRIAGE in the United States began with two court decisions that had nothing to do with gay couples. Years ago, many states had laws against interracial marriage. *Perez* and *Loving* changed that.

In 1947, Andrea Perez and Sylvester Davis, who had met while working at a defense plant in Los Angeles, applied for a marriage license. County Clerk W. G. Sharp refused their application because Perez was Mexican American and Davis was African American. The couple sued, and in 1948 the California Supreme Court ruled the state's miscegenation law unconstitutional.

The *Perez* decision only affected interracial couples in California. In 1958, Mildred and Richard Loving were arrested in their Virginia home for breaking that state's law. (They had been married in Washington, DC.) Rather than face jail time, they agreed to leave the state and not return for 25 years. But in 1963, after having three children, they wanted to move back to be near the rest of their family. They challenged the law.

The US Supreme Court eventually ruled in 1967 that all laws against interracial marriages were unconstitutional. Writing for the majority, Chief Justice Earl Warren stated, "The freedom to marry has long been recognized as one of the vital personal rights essential to the orderly pursuit of happiness by free men. Marriage is one of the 'basic civil rights of man,' fundamental to our very existence and survival."

Loving v. Virginia has been cited often in court rulings overturning same-sex marriage bans. On the 40th anniversary of the decision, Mildred Loving reflected on her legacy: "I am still not a political person, but I am proud that Richard's and my name is on a court case that can help reinforce the love, the commitment, the fairness, and the family that so many people, black or white, young or old, gay or straight, seek in life. I support the freedom to marry for all. That's what *Loving*, and loving, are all about."

trict was in San Francisco. During the speech Bush announced his opposition to same-sex marriage, even if that meant a constitutional amendment.

"I was disgusted," Newsom said. And even though he had been sworn into office just twelve days earlier, Newsom decided something needed to be done: he ordered the city clerk to begin issuing marriage licenses to same-sex couples. "I acted in order to honor my upbringing and my own marriage, support the commitment of real couples to form lifelong bonds, and defend the oath I took as mayor to protect liberty and justice for all, not just those of a certain class," he later wrote.

Shortly before noon on February 12, Phyllis Lyon and Del Martin, founders of the Daughters of Bilitis and partners for 51 years, received the first same-sex marriage license in California history, and then exchanged vows. "We thought they'd be the only couple married," Newsom admitted. "But the courts said there was no irreparable harm, so there was no temporary restraining order."

Word got out, and the rush was on. Before the end of the day, 89 other couples who had waited for hours in the rain tied the knot. More came the next day. But the day after that was a Saturday. And Valentine's Day. Would city hall be closed, as it usually was on the weekend?

Nope! Judges, clerks, clergy, and others volunteered to keep the doors open, and the line of couples with their families and friends stretched for blocks. Jennifer Nannini and Andrea Bourguet were among the crowd. Nannini recalled what happened while they waited for an official to marry them:

A volunteer approached us and asked if we wanted flowers for our ceremony. . . . She said they were being sent in from all over the country. Confused, I asked who they were for. "They're for you!" she said. Complete strangers sending flowers to show support for what we were about to do. Incredible. We picked out a beautiful bouquet of lilac roses and tulips. There was a card attached that said: "To a Loving Couple: Best wishes for a long and happy life together. Congratulations on your marriage. Bruce and Sue, Atlanta PFLAG."

The "Winter of Love" lasted 29 days before a judge ordered it stopped. In that span of time, a total of 4,037 couples married at city hall, where years earlier Harvey Milk and George Moscone had been murdered. Now there was a new chapter in the old building's history. For four weeks it had been, according to Mabel Teng, San Francisco's Assessor/Recorder, "the happiest place on earth."

And soon there were other happy places. Inspired by Newsom's move, the clerk of Sandoval County, New Mexico, began issuing marriage licenses to same-sex couples on February 20. Before a judge stepped in, 64 couples had gotten married. On February 27, the mayor of New Paltz, New York, presided over the wedding of 25 couples in his town. For a few days starting March 5, gay and lesbian couples could get licenses in Asbury Park, New Jersey. And over seven weeks starting March 3, more than 3,000 couples got licenses in Multnomah County, Oregon.

And then it ended. The California Supreme Court ruled on August 12, 2004, that all the licenses issued to same-sex couples in San Francisco were invalid. "Del is 83 years old and I am 79," Phyllis Lyon said at the time. "After being together for more than 50 years, it is a terrible blow to have the rights and protections of marriage taken away from us. At our age, we do not have the luxury of time."

They may not have had the luxury of time, but they had a marriage certificate. So did thousands of other couples. And those invalid certificates turned out to be just what they needed. But it would take some time.

Election Year Politics

ON FEBRUARY 24, 2004, two weeks after gays and lesbians started marrying in California, George W. Bush stood at a podium in the Roosevelt Room at the White House. "After more than two centuries of American jurisprudence, and millennia of human experience, a few judges and local authorities are presuming to change the most fundamental institution of civilization," he said. "Their actions have created confusion on an issue that requires clarity.... Activist courts have left the people with one recourse." He then called for a constitutional amendment defining marriage as

Teachers Derrick Tynan-Connolly and James Patrick Kennedy marry at San Francisco city hall, February 16, 2004. Photo by Daniel Nicoletta

only between one man and one woman. Bush concluded his remarks by saying, "We should also conduct this difficult debate in a matter worthy of our country, without bitterness or anger. In all that lies ahead, let us match strong convictions with kindness and good will and decency."

Very few people expected the debate to be polite. This was an election year, and many saw this as a maneuver by the Republicans to rally their conservative supporters and drive a wedge between the LGBT community and the Democrats.

A constitutional amendment is a difficult thing to pass, even when most people agree that it should pass. First, it must receive votes from two-thirds of both houses of Congress. Then, three-fourths of the state legislatures—38 of 50—would have to approve the amendment. How likely was that?

Not very. In fact, the amendment never made it past the first step. In the House of Representatives, it needed 290 votes to advance. It got only 227. The amendment didn't even get a *majority* in the Senate, much less the 67 votes (out of 100) that it needed. It failed 48–50, with two Democratic senators, John Kerry and John Edwards, abstaining. (To abstain means you don't vote either way—you pass.)

Kerry was running for president in 2004, and Edwards was his running mate. Both men had earlier said that they backed civil unions, not marriage. The LGBT community largely ignored the fact that Kerry and Edwards had abstained, for they realized it was mostly politics. Still, it was an unpleasant reminder that much of the Democratic Party didn't yet support full equality for gay and lesbian citizens.

And at the state level, things weren't much better. In the twelve months following the *Goodridge* decision, thirteen states amended their constitutions to ban same-sex marriage, and ten more followed in 2005 and 2006. It was legal overkill—all of those states already banned same-sex marriage.

Go, Canada!

WHILE THE UNITED STATES ARGUED OVER THE ISSUE OF SAME-SEX MARRIAGE, its neighbor to the north marched ahead without too much fanfare. Canada had always been more progressive on LGBT issues—the country legalized homosexuality in 1969, the same year as the Stonewall Uprising. In 1999, the Supreme Court of Canada ruled that same-sex couples should receive all the legal and financial benefits of marriage, though only heterosexual couples could use the word "marriage." But on June 10, 2003, the Court of Appeals for Ontario ruled that anything short of full equality violated the Canadian Charter of Rights and Freedoms. Michael Stark and Michael Leshner of Toronto were the first to tie the knot after the ruling. Seven provinces and the Yukon Territory joined Ontario during the next two years. And on July 20, 2005, the Parliament passed Bill C-38, which made same-sex civil marriage legal everywhere in Canada.

With Republicans on the attack, and the Democrats doing very little to stop them (and sometimes joining them), court challenges were still the best way for marriage equality supporters to go.

One State at a Time

"WILL YOU marry me?" Sean Fritz asked Tim McQuillan. Fritz was picking up McQuillan at work, and they were still sitting in the parking lot. Fritz held two rings and a single white rose. There were probably more romantic locations to pop the question, but things were moving fast. That afternoon, August 30, 2007, Iowa Judge Robert Hanson had ruled the state's ban on same-sex marriage unconstitutional. Fritz heard the news, immediately called McQuillan's mother to ask for her blessing, then raced out to the jewelry store.

McQuillan said yes, and they rushed to the Polk County recorder's office to get a license. The next morning, the couple asked for a waiver from the state's three-day waiting period, and before lunchtime the two were married by a Des Moines minister from the Unitarian Universalist Church.

Why the hurry? Everyone expected Judge Hanson's ruling to be appealed, and if it was appealed, marriages would be put on hold until a new decision was made. And that afternoon,

it was. No more licenses were issued. Even the six couples who had brought the lawsuit were not able to get married.

For the next 20 months, Fritz and McQuillan were Iowa's only married gay couple. Conservatives in the state legislature tried to pass a constitutional amendment against same-sex marriage, but failed, blocked by Democratic leaders. In April 2009, the Iowa Supreme Court unanimously agreed with the original decision, and marriages resumed. House Speaker Pat Murphy and Senate Majority Leader Michael Gronstal issued a joint statement:

When all is said and done, we believe the only lasting question about today's events will be why it took us so long. It is a tough question to answer because treating everyone fairly is really a matter of Iowa common sense and Iowa common decency.

Meanwhile, as the Iowa decision was being appealed, the lawsuit brought by couples whose "Winter of Love" marriages had been nullified reached the California Supreme Court. In a 4–3 decision on May 15, 2008, the justices declared the state's ban unconstitutional and ordered marriages to begin in June.

Once again, Phyllis Lyon and Del Martin became the first same-sex couple married in the state. At 5:01 PM on June 16, 2008, they both said

Del Martin (left) places a ring on Phyllis Lyon's finger while San Francisco mayor Gavin Newsom looks on, June 16, 2008. © Marcio Jose Sanchez/AP/Corbis

"I do" in a brief ceremony conducted by San Francisco mayor Gavin Newsom.

Two months later, on August 27, Del Martin passed away, survived by her wife of 10 weeks or 55 years, depending on how one counted.

Prop 8

STILL, THE fight in California was far from over. Expecting to lose in court, an alliance of churches and conservative organizations was planning a new strategy. The group, called Protect Marriage, began collecting signatures to put a measure on the 2008 ballot—Proposition 8—that would ban gay marriage. Again.

The "Yes On 8" campaign was slick and expensive. Much of the money came from the Mormon Church and its followers, as well as the Catholic Church. It was perfectly legal for any citizen to contribute to the campaign, or against it, but some questioned why churches could claim tax-free status yet contribute to a political campaign.

California voters were bombarded with television and radio ads from both sides. "Yes On 8" did its best to play on parents' emotions. One television commercial showed a young girl telling her mother, "Guess what I learned in school today. I learned how a prince married a prince, and I can marry a princess!" The ad went on to say that without Prop 8, same-sex marriage would be part of the school curriculum. Other commercials claimed that all churches would be forced to perform same-sex marriages. Neither was true.

The fear campaign worked. In November, Prop 8 was approved 52–48 percent. Same-sex marriages immediately stopped. It was the first time in history a state had changed its constitution to take away marriage rights from citizens who were legally marrying. It was a particularly hard blow for the LGBT community, since California voters also overwhelmingly approved another measure, Prop 2, which mandated that farmers treat their chickens more humanely (among other things).

People took to the streets in California and nationwide. On November 15, more than 12,000 protested at Los Angeles city hall. Another 5,000 rallied outside the Salt Lake Temple in Utah. Even more expressed their outrage through social media and online campaigns.

One of the most visible online protests was the NOH8 ("No Hate") Campaign. Celebrity photographer Adam Bouska and his partner Jeff Parshley posted photos of everyday Californians, their mouths covered with duct tape to symbolize voices silenced by the measure. It quickly grew, and soon movie stars, musicians, lawmakers, and artists joined the effort.

The message was clear: *This fight was NOT over.*

Change in Washington

OF COURSE, the 2008 election wasn't just about California's Proposition 8. On November 4, the American public elected a new president,

Barack Obama. The LGBT community supported Obama in large numbers, even though during the campaign he said he supported civil unions instead of marriage for gay and lesbian couples. Obama did, however, endorse many issues dear to the hearts of LGBT voters, such

Out actor Jane Lynch was one of thousands to participate in the NOH8 Campaign. Photo by Adam Bouska, courtesy NOH8 Campaign (noh8campaign.com)

"VOTE" ON A PROPOSITION

DO YOU KNOW how propositions make it onto the ballot in *your* state? And how your state's constitution can be amended? Every state is different. Research how both of these processes work for your community—start by visiting the website for your Secretary of State or Board of Elections. Try to find answers to the following questions:

Propositions

1. Does your state allow citizens to put propositions on the ballot? (Some do. Some don't.)

2. If so, do citizens collect signatures on a petition? How many signatures are needed?

3. Or does the state legislature control ballot measures, where they are only placed on the ballot by elected representatives, not citizens?

4. Now find a ballot (online) from a recent election, or one from an upcoming election, where at least one proposition is included. How would *you* vote on the proposition(s) if you could?

Constitutional Amendments

1. Can citizens amend their state's constitution, or only the legislature?

2. If the citizens can, is it by a simple majority vote?

3. If the legislature amends the constitution, what is the process?

4. Has your state amended its constitution recently? If so, what changed?

© Visions of America LLC

as the repeal of both Don't Ask, Don't Tell and the Defense of Marriage Act.

Halting the collapse of the economy was the first item on Obama's plate. But in the spring, he appointed John Berry, an openly gay man, as director of the Office of Personnel Management (OPM). For years the OPM (and its predecessor, the US Civil Service Commission) had enforced the no-gays-in-government rule. At a formal ceremony on June 24, 2009, Berry gave a written apology to Frank Kameny for his firing 52 years earlier. With tears in his eyes, Kameny choked out, "Apology accepted." Kameny was then given the Teddy Roosevelt Award, the highest service honor given to federal employees.

The award topped off a busy few years for Kameny. In 2005, he and Barbara Gittings were on hand for the unveiling of a historic marker in Philadelphia honoring the Annual Reminders outside Independence Hall. In 2006, he donated his personal papers to the Library of Congress, and in 2008, the Smithsonian accepted his picket signs from the Annual Reminders to put on display. In 2009, his home at 5020 Cathedral Avenue was named a DC Historic Landmark. The same year, he was given the pen Obama used to sign a presidential memorandum giving expanded benefits to the same-sex partners of federal employees.

President Obama also made headway on the problem of hate crimes. On October 28, 2009, the president signed the Matthew Shepard and James Byrd Jr. Hate Crimes Prevention Act into law. (Byrd was an African American resident of Jasper, Texas, who was brutally murdered by three white supremacists on June 7, 1998.) Both the Byrd and Shepard families attended the signing. Under the new law, the federal government can charge a suspect with a hate crime if local law enforcement can't make such a charge or refuses to do so. Many states do not have hate crimes laws.

A New Kind of Backlash

SUPPORTERS OF Prop 8 probably didn't realize how it would energize the LGBT community, not just in California but across the nation. In the years following Prop 8's passage, almost every state saw a legal challenge to its marriage laws.

Several state legislatures decided not to wait for judges to make the decision for them. Pushed by increasingly impatient LGBT voters and their supporters, lawmakers acted. In early April 2009, the Vermont general assembly passed a marriage equality bill. Later that month, the Connecticut legislature did the same. New Hampshire and the District of Columbia also changed their marriage laws in 2009.

California couples weren't waiting either. In spring 2009, a federal lawsuit was filed by Ted Olson and David Boies, lawyers for the Ameri-

President Barack Obama shakes Frank Kameny's hand in the Oval Office after signing a presidential memorandum on June 17, 2009.

© Larry Downing/Reuters/Corbis

can Foundation for Equal Rights, on behalf of two couples—Kristin Perry and Sandy Stier, and Jeffrey Zarrillo and Paul Katami. California's elected officials refused to defend Prop 8 in court, leaving it to the Protect Marriage organization to defend the law. It did not go well for them.

The 12-day trial began in January 2010. Protect Marriage soon learned that the wild accusations they'd made during the political campaign would not hold up in a court of law.

They would have to support their claims with evidence, and they had very little. For example, one of the leaders of "Yes On 8," William Tam, had claimed that just a few years after legalizing same-sex marriage, the Netherlands had done the same with polygamy—the marriage of one man to multiple wives. (It had not.) When asked where he found this information, Tam replied, "It's in the Internet." David Boies was even able to get one of Protect Marriage's star witnesses to state, "I believe that adopting same-sex marriage would be likely to improve the well-being of gay and lesbian households and their children."

On August 4, 2010, Judge Vaughn Walker ruled that Prop 8 was unconstitutional on the grounds of equal protection—gay citizens were being treated differently than their heterosexual neighbors—and due process—that the law was unfair and unreasonable. The decision was immediately appealed to a higher court, and in time would reach the US Supreme Court.

The Prop 8 team (from left to right) outside the US Supreme Court: plaintiffs Kristin Perry and Sandy Stier, lawyers Ted Olson and David Boies, and plaintiffs Paul Katami and Jeffrey Zarrillo.

© Jim Lo Scalzo/EPA/Corbis

The End of Don't Ask, Don't Tell

IN THE decade following the enactment of Don't Ask, Don't Tell (DADT), the US military discharged thousands of gay and lesbian servicemembers. This included dozens of Arabic translators, vital positions that the Pentagon could never find enough people to fill.

The LGBT community had been fighting DADT since 1993, but it was a long, uphill battle. Some lobbied Congress to overturn the policy, but these were the same lawmakers who had put it in place—nobody was going to change their minds anytime soon. And despite the need for recruits to serve in Afghanistan and Iraq, President Bush said he would not change the policy.

The only strategy that looked promising was through the courts. But because the military has its own court system, judges in civilian (regular) courts are reluctant to make sweeping decisions that affect the Pentagon. Several veterans discharged under DADT sued to return to active duty, or have their discharges changed to "honorable" and allow them to retire with full benefits. A few won, though the decisions only applied to their particular cases.

At the time Barack Obama was elected in 2008, polls showed most Americans wanted DADT repealed. Nevertheless, the president said it might be years before it was overturned. So gay veterans ramped up the pressure. On March 18, 2010, former army officers Dan Choi and Jim Pietrangelo chained themselves to the White House fence in protest. On April 20 they returned with four more vets and did it again.

Then, on September 9, 2010, a federal judge in California ruled that DADT was unconstitutional. Though the decision was put on hold while it was appealed, it now looked like the policy would end without any input of Congress, the president, or the Pentagon. And none of them wanted that.

Unfortunately, an election was just two months away, and it was easier to argue about it than to change anything. After the election, there were even more Republicans who opposed repeal, but they wouldn't take office until January. Then, in one of its last votes on the 2010 calendar, Congress repealed DADT.

The policy didn't end immediately—the Pentagon was allowed to "certify" when it was ready for DADT to end. It took almost a year, but on September 20, 2011, the destructive policy came to an end. According to Servicemembers United, an organization for LGBT military, during the eighteen years DADT was in effect, 14,346 soldiers, sailors, and airmen/women had been discharged.

It Gets Better

AS CHILDREN returned to school in fall 2010, there was a disturbing number of teen suicides reported across the nation. Columnist and political commentator Dan Savage wrote about two victims, Justin Aaberg of Anoka, Minnesota, and Billy Lucas of Greensburg, Indiana. Both had been mercilessly bullied by their classmates and neighbors.

One of Savage's readers posted a comment: "My heart breaks for the pain and torment you went through, Billy Lucas. I wish I could have told you that things get better."

That was it! Savage realized. "Why are we waiting for permission to talk to these kids?" he thought. "We have the ability to talk directly to them right now. We don't have to wait for permission to let them know that *it gets better*. We can reach these kids."

Savage called his husband Terry Miller, who loved the idea. The couple soon recorded a heartfelt video of the bullying they'd experienced growing up, but more importantly, the wonderful things that had happened to them since then: their marriage, and adoption of a son. On September 21, they posted it to YouTube. And it exploded.

In two weeks, the It Gets Better Project exceeded YouTube's 650-video limit, which had to be expanded. Before year's end, thousands had submitted videos, including Barack and Michelle Obama, Hillary Clinton, Neil Patrick Harris, Lady Gaga, Stephen Colbert, the Chicago Cubs, and Kermit the Frog. Today there are more than 50,000 online videos that have been viewed more than 50 million times.

Many of the people in the videos encouraged viewers to contact the Trevor Project if they felt they wanted to harm themselves. The organization grew out of *Trevor*, a film that won the 1995 Academy Award for Best Short Subject. The movie is about a 13-year-old who tries to kill himself after his middle-school crush rejects him and his classmates learn he is gay. The filmmakers were concerned that viewers might get the wrong message, so they set up the Trevor Lifeline, a phone hotline for anyone who might be depressed.

After the attention it got from the It Gets Better Project, the lifeline needed to expand its operations. It opened a third call center in Harvey Milk's old camera shop in San Francisco.

Freedom Spreads

ON A sunny day, you can often see a rainbow in the mist rising from Niagara Falls. But on July 24, 2011, you could see a rainbow in the

Terry Miller (left) and Dan Savage on the first It Gets Better video, September 2010.
Courtesy It Gets Better

dead of night. The entire chasm was lit up like an enormous pride flag. Standing just feet from the tumbling waters on the New York side, Niagara Falls mayor Paul Dyster began the ceremony at 12:01 AM. Within moments, Kitty Lambert and Cheryle Rudd became the first same-sex couple married in the state. Before the end of the day, hundreds more would marry as well.

The change in New York's marriage law had been made by the state legislature, not by a court order. After several unsuccessful attempts, starting in 2007, the law eventually made it through and was signed into law by the governor.

The Obama administration was also making changes. At the end of the year, Secretary of State Hillary Clinton had made LGBT rights a central theme of her speech to the United Nations on Human Rights Day. "Gay rights are human rights, and human rights are gay rights," she said, and promised that the United States would push countries to improve their policies for their LGBT citizens.

And yet some thought it hypocritical for the Obama administration to be lecturing others when, at the time, the president didn't support marriage equality. Then Vice President Joe Biden spoke up. As a guest on *Meet the Press* in May 2012, Biden was asked about his own feeling about same-sex marriage. "I am absolutely

STOP THE BULLYING

BULLYING has long been a school problem. Fortunately, most schools have adopted programs and policies to prevent it, or to correct the problem if it happens. Students are bullied for many reasons—not just because they may be LGBT—but none of them are justified.

What does your school do to prevent bullying? If you don't know, ask. Here are three national antibullying campaigns in which you or your school can participate.

Spirit Day: Every year on the third Thursday in October (National Bullying Prevention Month), students are asked to wear purple to show their support for LGBT youth. Spirit Day was started in 2010 by Canadian teenager Brittany McMillan after several LGBT suicides. She chose purple because it represents "spirit" on the rainbow flag. Today it is sponsored by GLAAD, the Gay & Lesbian Alliance Against Defamation. Visit www.glaad.org /spiritday for more information.

National Day of Silence: In 1996, Maria Pulzetti asked students at the University of Virginia to take a one-day vow of silence to draw attention to those silenced by bullying. Today the National Day of Silence is held in mid-April, and is sponsored by the Gay, Lesbian & Straight Education Network. See www.dayofsilence .org for this year's date.

Athlete Ally Pledge: The organization Athlete Ally (www.athleteally.org) promotes the values of respect and inclusion. If you play sports, you're encouraged to take the organization's pledge:

I pledge to lead my athletic community to respect and welcome all persons, regardless of their perceived or actual sexual orientation, gender identity, or gender expression. Beginning right now, I will do my part to promote the best of athletics by making all players feel respected on and off the field.

comfortable with the fact that men marrying men, women marrying women, and heterosexual men and women marrying [one] another are entitled to the same exact rights, all the civil rights, all the civil liberties," he said. "And quite frankly, I don't see much of a distinction beyond that."

Biden's comments put him at odds with the president, and the press began hounding the White House for clarification. Three days later, Obama told reporter Robin Roberts, "At a certain point, I've just concluded that—for me personally, it is important for me to go ahead and affirm that—I think same-sex couples should be able to get married." He then credited his daughters with changing his mind. "It wouldn't dawn on them that somehow their friends' parents would be treated differently. It doesn't make sense to them and frankly, that's the kind of thing that prompts a change in perspective."

At that moment, the 2012 presidential race was in full swing, and nobody knew whether Obama's change of heart would hurt or help him at the ballot box. Republican candidate Mitt Romney reminded reporters that he did not support same-sex marriage, and he didn't support civil unions either.

"The president, I think, has handed to Mitt Romney the one missing piece in his campaign," claimed Tony Perkins of the Family Research Council. "That is the intensity and motivation that Mitt Romney needs among social conservatives to win this election."

That November voters in Washington, Maryland, and Maine were also being asked to decide whether to extend marriage to gay and lesbian couples. On the marriage question, the LGBT community had lost almost every time up through 2008. But in 2012? They won in Maine. They won in Maryland. They won in Washington. And Barack Obama was elected to a second term. And an even greater victory was just a few months away.

Edith Windsor Slays the DOMA Dragon

ON JUNE 28, 1969, Thea Spyer and Edith Windsor were in Greenwich Village near the Stonewall Inn. They had just arrived in New York from a vacation in Europe, and hadn't heard what happened just hours earlier. Police were everywhere.

Though they were part of the LGBT world at the time, they weren't always comfortable with some in the community, like drag queens. "I [didn't] wanna be identified with them," Windsor later admitted. But then she learned what had happened that night, and who had fought the hardest at the uprising. "From then on . . . I felt this incredible gratitude. They changed my life. You know, they changed my life forever, those queens." It was more than 40 years before Edith Windsor could return the favor. And what she did was every bit as monumental as Stonewall.

Windsor and Spyer had met in 1963, and became a couple in 1965. Spyer later proposed to Windsor, but, worried that her coworkers would learn their secret, Windsor wore a circular diamond pin rather than an engagement ring.

In 1977, Spyer was diagnosed with multiple sclerosis (MS), an often disabling disease of the central nervous system. It didn't immediately stop her from working, or prevent the couple from having many happy years together. But over the decades, her MS got progressively worse. In 2007 she was told that she had less than a year to live, so she asked Windsor if she still wanted to get married. Windsor did. They flew to Toronto, Canada, and married on May 22, 2007. It had been a long engagement—they had already been together for 42 years.

Spyer lived for two more years, and died at home on February 5, 2009. Within a month, Windsor had a heart attack. And then she learned she would be taxed $363,053 on her "inheritance" from Spyer. Of course, it wasn't an inheritance at all—it was everything the couple had built and saved together as a couple. But according to the Defense of Marriage Act (DOMA), the federal government didn't recog-

nize their perfectly legal Canadian marriage. Windsor was taxed as if Spyer was a mere acquaintance, not her wife. (Spouses pay no inheritance tax.)

So Windsor hired lawyer Roberta Kaplan and sued. The case moved through two lower courts, and she won both times. It was finally heard by the US Supreme Court on March 27, 2013. Once the case was presented, there was nothing to do but wait for a decision.

Three states, however, did not wait. In May, legislatures in Rhode Island, Delaware, and Minnesota all voted to legalize same-sex marriage, and their governors signed the bills.

The US Supreme Court in 2013. Front row (left to right), Clarence Thomas, Antonin Scalia, Chief Justice John Roberts, Anthony Kennedy, and Ruth Bader Ginsberg; Back row (left to right), Sonia Sotomayor, Stephen Breyer, Samuel Alito, and Elena Kagan. Steve Petteway, Collection of the Supreme Court of the United States

Then, on June 26, 2013, the high court handed down two decisions. In the Prop 8 case, the justices said the supporters of Prop 8 had no right to appeal the lower court's decision when the law was declared unconstitutional. Prop 8 was dead.

The decision in Windsor's case was far more important. In a 5–4 ruling, the Supreme Court struck down most of DOMA. Writing for the majority, Justice Kennedy said, "DOMA undermines both the public and private significance of state-sanctioned same-sex marriages; for it tells those couples, and all the world, that their otherwise valid marriages are unworthy of federal recognition." He detailed all the federal benefits denied same-sex couples because of DOMA, and added his thoughts about the affect it had on their families: "[It] humiliates tens of thousands of children now being raised by same-sex couples. The law in question makes it even more difficult for the children to understand the integrity and closeness of their own family."

Justice Scalia disagreed, and predicted that the ruling would have far-reaching consequences: "As far as this Court is concerned, no one should be fooled; it is just a matter of listening and waiting for the other shoe. . . . [T]he majority arms well every challenger to a state law restricting marriage to its traditional definition." Marriage equality would spread nationwide, and there was little anyone could do to stop it.

Two days after the rulings, same-sex marriages resumed in California. The first couple to tie the knot was Kristin Perry and Sandra Stier, who had brought the case. Their wedding was held at San Francisco city hall, just feet from a statue of Harvey Milk. Later that day,

Edith Windsor greets a cheering crowd outside the US Supreme Court after her case is heard on March 27, 2013. The circular diamond engagement pin given to her by Thea Spyer is on her jacket. © Pete Marovich/Corbis

Jeffrey Zarrillo and Paul Katami were married by Los Angeles mayor Antonio Villaraigosa.

Decisions, Decisions

FOLLOWING THE victories at the Supreme Court, judges across the United States began striking down state bans on same-sex marriage. Many directly cited the *United States v. Windsor* case, often quoting the dissent written by Antonin Scalia.

New Jersey was the first to fall on September 27, 2013. The state's Republican governor, Chris Christie, fought the ruling and lost. Just after midnight on October 21, couples started marrying.

In November, with lawsuits breathing down their necks, state legislatures in Hawaii and Illinois passed bills legalizing same-sex marriage. Hawaii couples could start marrying in December, but Illinois gays and lesbians would have to wait until the following June.

On December 19, 2013, the New Mexico State Supreme Court struck down the state's ban. A day later, Utah's law was declared unconstitutional. After the New Year came more rulings—week after week after week—and all in favor of equality. On January 14, Oklahoma. February 13, Virginia. Texas… Michigan… Arkansas… Idaho… all were decided by spring, and each overturned state bans.

Because most of these rulings were made by federal judges at the state level, they could be appealed to higher courts—district courts, where several states in a region are grouped together, and eventually the US Supreme Court. When a ruling is appealed, the decision made by the lower court is usually put on hold. In other words, couples in those states couldn't be married just yet.

Illinois governor Pat Quinn signs the Religious Freedom and Marriage Fairness Bill, November 20, 2013. Photo by author

But that was not the case everywhere. Nobody had to wait in Oregon after a judge overturned its ban on May 19, nor in Pennsylvania the following day, when that state's law prohibiting gay marriage was thrown out. "We are a better people than what these laws represent," wrote Judge John Jones III in his Pennsylvania decision, "and it is time to discard them into the ash heap of history." Couples began marrying immediately.

In June, marriage bans in Wisconsin and Indiana fell. In July, Kentucky. And Colorado. And Florida. By September, eleven of these state cases had been appealed to the US Supreme Court. Then on October 6, 2014, the high court shocked everyone: it refused to hear any of the cases! Because all of the lower courts generally agreed that the laws were unconstitutional, there wasn't much for the justices to discuss. And when the Supreme Court turns down an appeal, the lower court ruling stands. On the day before the announcement, there were 19 states (and the District of Columbia) where gay and lesbian couples could marry. Now there were 30.

A week later, two more were added—Alaska and Arizona. And then Missouri. And Mississippi. In 2015, South Dakota and Alabama.

Then, in 2015, the US Supreme Court agreed to take up the issue of whether states can ban gay marriage. The case was known as *Obergefell v. Hodges*. Just after the Windsor decision was announced in 2013, James Obergefell and John Arthur decided to marry. Arthur was suffering from ALS (Lou Gehrig's disease) and did not have long to live. The Cincinnati couple chartered a medical transport plane to fly them to Maryland where they were legally married on the airport tarmac, then flew back to Ohio.

Three months later, Arthur died. The state of Ohio refused to list him as married on the death certificate, so husband Jim Obergefell sued to have the state ban overturned. The case was eventually decided on June 26, 2015. Writing for the majority in the 5–4 decision, Justice Anthony Kennedy said:

No union is more profound than marriage, for it embodies the highest ideals of love, fidelity, devotion, sacrifice, and family. In forming a marital union, two people become something greater than once they were. . . . [M]arriage embodies a love that may endure even past death. It would misunderstand these men and women to say they disrespect the idea of marriage. Their plea is that they do respect it, respect it so deeply that they seek to find its fulfillment for themselves. Their hope is not to be condemned to live in loneliness, excluded from one of civilization's oldest institutions. They ask for equal dignity in the eyes of the law. The Constitution grants them that right.

Four justices dissented, but at this point, it didn't much matter—marriage equality was now the law of the land. Everywhere. From sea to shining sea.

What Next?

IT WOULD be easy to think that the fight for LGBT equality in the United States is nearly won. But as of this book's publication, it is still perfectly legal to fire somebody for being gay or lesbian in 29 states—more than half the country. Transgender people are at risk in 32 states. The same is true for public accommodations and housing. An LGBT customer can be denied service at a restaurant or be turned away at a hotel, and there is nothing he or she can do about it.

There is also the problem of employment discrimination. First introduced to Congress in 1994, the Employment Non-Discrimination Act would make it illegal to fire someone because of their sexual orientation or gender identity, the same way a person cannot be fired for their race or sex. Twenty years later, it has yet to pass.

The visibility of the transgender community is also growing. In June 2014 actress Laverne Cox appeared on the cover of *Time* magazine beside the headline, THE TRANSGENDER TIPPING POINT—AMERICA'S NEXT CIVIL RIGHTS FRONTIER. And in the spring of 2015, the world learned that the Olympic decathlon champion Bruce Jenner was transitioning and would now be known as Caitlyn Jenner. Still, the community has much to overcome to achieve full equality and acceptance.

And what about the rest of the world? The LGBT community enjoys more protections and rights in Western Europe than it does in the United States, but LGBT people are widely persecuted in Eastern Europe, Africa, and Asia. Some countries in Central and South America have laws protecting gays and lesbians, but most do not. Their struggle is just beginning.

There is still so much to do before we reach full equality. But two things should be perfectly clear after reading this history. First, the LGBT community has never given up on a struggle, even if it took decades to achieve. And second, in the end, they always win.

▲ ▼ ▲

"Never doubt that a small group of thoughtful citizens can change the world. Indeed, it's the only thing that ever has."

—Margaret Mead

Everyday Heroes

As you've learned, the long fight for LGBT civil rights is filled with stories of women, men, and children who stood up to injustice against remarkable odds, and won. There is no shortage of heroes—you could probably find some in your own community, or family.

Theresa Volpe and Mercedes Santos, whose story opened this book, weren't looking to be heroes. Like any parents, their first concern was their children. It just happened that what was best for their children involved a whole lot more than what happened at the hospital in 2011. Yet that is where this story resumes.

Mercedes left the intensive care unit and eventually found Theresa. Getting nowhere, they turned to one another and said, "Let's just go in." But then a hospital administrator arrived, and after explaining the situation once more, both were admitted into the room with Jaidon. His condition eventually improved, but it would be another two weeks before he recovered and could go home.

Theresa and Mercedes couldn't help but wonder, *What if this happens again?* The hospital had treated their family the same way their own government did. They were second-class citizens. None of this would have happened if they had been married, and they couldn't get married because they were both women.

Word of their story reached Lambda Legal, a civil rights organization that was hoping to challenge the ban on same-sex marriage in Illinois. The group reached out to the couple,

◀ **Theresa Volpe and son Jaidon at the Illinois Capitol Building in Springfield.** REUTERS/Jim Young (RTXXX4U)

and eventually they joined a lawsuit to overturn the ban. Sixteen couples from across the state joined the Lambda Legal lawsuit, as well as nine more couples who were part of a parallel suit brought by the American Civil Liberties Union.

Legal cases don't typically move quickly through the courts; they can take years to resolve. So while the two lawsuits crept along, LGBT activists and politicians worked to change the law through the state legislature.

Over the next two years, the Santos-Volpe family made many trips to the state capitol in Springfield to lobby senators and representatives. In January 2013, they testified before the Senate Executive Committee considering the marriage equality bill. With Mercedes, Ava, and Jaidon by her side, Theresa spoke for the family. She recalled what had happed two years earlier, and why the bill mattered. "Our children want us to be married," she concluded. "We want to feel secure that we can protect them and be there for them when they need us. We want them to understand that their family is just as worthy of respect as any other Illinois family."

The bill passed in the Senate on Valentine's Day, but got bogged down in the House of Representatives during the spring. LGBT activists and community leaders turned up the heat, and so did the opposition. Both sides marched and protested. They wrote letters to newspapers and politicians. And finally, on November 5, 2013, the bill came up for a vote in the House. Nobody knew for sure if it would pass. The Santos-Volpe family watched the debate from the balcony, and grabbed each other's hands when the vote was called: 61 yeas, 54 nays. They won!

At the end of the day, the family was invited to the Illinois governor's mansion for a victory reception. There, Ava and Jaidon's mothers showed them paintings of Abraham Lincoln and told them how they, too, were now part of Illinois history.

Santos and Volpe would be the first to point out how many people fought to make marriage equality a reality in Illinois—activists and concerned citizens, lawyers and plaintiffs, legislators and lobbyists, and thousands of people who marched, protested, and pressured their elected representatives. So many people, in fact, that when it came time to sign the bill on November 20, their family wasn't invited onto the crowded stage.

It was probably for the best, because Theresa and Mercedes had their hands full. Eight days earlier, Theresa had given birth to their third child, Lennox. The family did have a front-row seat, however, as the governor signed the bill into law while sitting at a desk once owned by Abraham Lincoln. An overflow crowd of thousands watched and cheered and cried.

Things have gotten back to normal at the Santos-Volpe household—"normal" being carpools to Ava's basketball practices, out-of-town swim meets, math team, and piano and fiddle lessons; Jaidon's chess tournaments, karate practice, and piano lessons; and Lennox's mommy-and-baby music classes. And school. And homework.

But everything isn't as it was before. It's better. Theresa and Mercedes see it in their children, who look at the world differently. They want the world to be fair, or at least fairer. And because of their mothers, they know it's possible. "If we didn't stand up for our rights," Theresa and Mercedes asked each other years earlier, "How could we expect them to?"

▲ ▼ ▲

Acknowledgments

I'VE NEVER had this much fun researching and writing a book. Every time I explained the subject to a librarian, archivist, photographer, or veteran of the LGBT struggle, he or she assisted me with an enthusiasm I've never before experienced—without exception. They opened their files, made suggestions, and pointed me in new and interesting directions. Thank you all, in particular Theresa Volpe and Mercedes Santos, Dan Nicoletta, Suzanne Manford Swan, Pat Rocco, Rachelle Lee Smith, and Mark Segal. Also, Carlos Alcala (Communications Director for Assemblyman Tom Ammiano); Crystal Miles and Teresa Mora (Bancroft Library); Katherine Lynch (Bletchley Park); Joy Novak and Carol Wells (Center for the Study of Political Graphics); Marjorie Bryer (GLBT Historical Society); Ianthe Metzger (Human Rights Campaign); Sara David (It Gets Better Project); Rich Wandel (LGBT Community Center National History Archive); Jörg Litwinschuh and Sophie Richter (Magnus Hirschfeld Foundation); Meg Costello (Museums on the Green); Andrea Felder, Thomas Lisanti, Tal Nadan, and David Rosado (New York Public Library); Chris Hayden (NOH8 Campaign); Yesenia Martinez, Kyle Morgan, Michael Oliveira, and Loni Shibuyama (ONE Archives at USC Libraries); Liz Owen (PFLAG); Jonathan Silin (Robert Giard Foundation); Mike Levy, Christina Moretta, and Jeff Thomas (San Francisco Public Library); Diana Carey (Schlesinger Library); Adam Minakowski and Daisy Njoku (Smithsonian Institution); Duncan Knox and Steve Petteway (Supreme Court of the United States); Yuriy Shcherbina (USC Digital Libraries); and Will Wilson (Vicksburg National Military Park).

At Chicago Review Press, Cynthia Sherry championed this project from the beginning, and I can't thank her enough. I must also acknowledge the hard work and talent poured into this book's development and design by Ellen Hornor, Amelia Estrich, Monica Baziuk, Jon Hahn, and Allison Felus.

On a personal level, I am indebted to those who helped me on my own journey as a writer—Kathy Royer, Bonnie Papke, Robert Johnson, Aimee Strawn, and David Page—and a happy gay man—Tess and Juan; Henrique, Pat, Paul, and David; and my fellow volunteers with the Horizons Youth Group.

To my parents, brothers, and their spouses and wonderful children, I owe so much. And to my husband, Jim, all my love.

▲ ▼ ▲

Books to Read

Alsenas, Linas. *Gay America: Struggle for Equality*. New York: Amulet Books, 2008.

Bausum, Ann. *Stonewall: Breaking Out in the Fight for Gay Rights*. New York: Viking, 2015.

Kaufman, Moisés, and the Members of the Tectonic Theater Project. *The Laramie Project*. New York: Vintage Books, 2001.

Lecesne, James. *Trevor*. New York: Seven Stories Press, 2012.

Marcus, Eric. *Making Gay History: The Half-Century Fight for Lesbian and Gay Equal Rights*. New York: HarperCollins, 2002.

Savage, Dan, and Terry Miller, eds. *It Gets Better: Coming Out, Overcoming Bullying, and Creating a Life Worth Living*. New York: Dutton, 2011.

Setterington, Ken. *Branded by the Pink Triangle*. Toronto: Second Story Press, 2013.

Smith, Rachelle Lee. *Speaking Out*. Oakland, CA: PM Press, 2014.

Movies to See

Common Threads: Stories from the Quilt (1989)

How to Survive a Plague (2012)

No Secret Anymore: The Times of Del Martin & Phyllis Lyon (2003)

Out of the Past (1997)

Pride (2014)

The Times of Harvey Milk (1984)

Places to Visit

The Center
208 W. 13th Street
New York, New York 10011
(212) 620-7310
https://gaycenter.org/archives
Visit the place where ACT UP, Queer Nation, and other LGBT organizations began. In addition to educational programs, the Center is home to the LGBT Community Center National History Archives.

Christopher Park
Christopher, Grove, and W. Fourth Streets
New York, New York 10014
www.nycgovparks.org/parks
/christopherpark
Located just across the street from the Stonewall Inn, Christopher Park has a sculpture by George Segal titled *Gay Liberation Monument* which celebrates the LGBT community.

Gerber/Hart Library and Archives
6500 N. Clark Street
Chicago, Illinois 60616
(312) 381-8030
www.gerberhart.org
Though primarily a research and lending library, the Gerber/Hart has display cases filled with interesting items from its collection, as well as book groups and programs for the LGBT community.

The GLBT History Museum
4127 18th Street
San Francisco, California 94114
(415) 621-1107
www.glbthistory.org/museum/index.html
This museum focuses on San Francisco's unique contributions to the LGBT civil rights movement, including archives and artifacts from the Daughters of Bilitis, José Sarria, Harvey Milk, and more.

The Legacy Walk
3200–3700 N. Halsted Street
Chicago, Illinois 60613
www.legacyprojectchicago.org
This five-block outdoor memorial honors dozens of LGBT pioneers, organizations, and movements. If you can't make it to Chicago, its informational plaques are available to view online.

The NAMES Foundation
AIDS Memorial Quilt
204 14 Street NW
Atlanta, Georgia 30318
(404) 688-5500
www.aidsquilt.org
Each year the NAMES Foundation stages more than 1,000 displays of the AIDS Memorial Quilt across the nation and world. Check the schedule on the website—find out if the Quilt will be coming to your town or somewhere near it in the future.

National LGBT Museum
PO Box 1975, New York, NY 10113
http://nationallgbtmuseum.org
Currently in development, this museum will eventually open in New York City. Check the website to track its progress, and see its plans for the first national museum dedicated to the LGBT community.

ONE Archives Foundation
909 W. Adams Boulevard
Los Angeles, California 90007
(213) 821-2771
www.onearchives.org/traveling-history
  -exhibitions/
The ONE Archives has many traveling exhibitions on LGBT history available for schools, libraries, businesses, and cultural institutions.

Notes

Introduction

All quotes, interview with Theresa Volpe and Mercedes Santos, November 21, 2014.

Chapter 1

"It was then and there" Lynn Sherr, *America the Beautiful* (New York: Public Affairs, 2001), 34.

"Greetings from Pikes Peak" Ibid., 37.

"A better American" Ibid., 29.

"one soul together" Paula Martinac, *The Queerest Places* (New York: Henry Holt, 1997), 37.

"did not care for women" R. B. Parkinson, *A Little Gay History* (New York: Columbia University Press, 2013), 15.

"Society has had recently" Will Roscoe, *The Zuni Man-Woman* (Albuquerque: University of New Mexico Press, 1991), 56.

"universal regret and distress" Ibid., 4.

"I have fallen in love" Michael Bronski, *A Queer History of the United States* (Boston: Beacon Press, 2011), 73.

"We were familiar at once" Frank Muzzy, *Gay and Lesbian Washington, DC* (Mount Pleasant, SC: Arcadia, 2005), 17.

"with my love" Keith Stern, *Queers in History* (Dallas, TX: BenBella Books, 2009), 489.

"I now and then put it on" Rodger Streitmatter, *Outlaw Marriages* (Boston: Beacon Press, 2012), 10.

"Howard's ancestral family" Charles H. Hughes, "Marriages Between Women," *Alienist and Neurologist* 23, no. 4 (November 1902), 498–500.

"Miss Nancy" and "Aunt Fancy" Jean H. Baker, *James Buchanan* (New York: Times Books, 2004), 25.

"I am now 'solitary and alone'" Robert Watson, *Affairs of State* (New York: Rowman & Littlefield, 2012), 246.

"male-bodied person" Jim Burroway, "Today's Birthday: Karl Heinrich Ulrichs," Box Turtle Bulletin, August 28, 2014, www.boxturtle bulletin.com/2014/08/28/66711#1825.

"female-bodied person" Ibid.

"the most depraved man" John Lauritsen and David Thorstad, *The Early Homosexual Rights Movement* (New York: Times Change Press, 1974), 53.

"Gentlemen of the jury" Ibid., 55.

"The world is growing more tolerant" Moisés Kaufman, *Gross Indecency* (New York: Vintage, 1998), 122.

"This is the worst case" Ibid., 126.

Chapter 2

"It is funny that men" Gertrude Stein, *Wars I Have Seen* (New York: Random House, 1945), 12.

"I regard it as a tragedy" Lauritsen and Thorstad, *The Early Homosexual Rights Movement*, 37.

"were often of finer grain" Martinac, *The Queerest Places*, 310.

"You must know, dear" Streitmatter, *Outlaw Marriages*, 37.

"Through science to justice" Ralf Dose, *Magnus Hirschfeld* (New York: Monthly Review Press, 2014), 8.

"The film you are about" Paul Russell, *The Gay 100* (New York: Kensington Books, 1995), 17.

"The first difficulty was" Jonathan Ned Katz, *Gay American History* (New York: Avon, 1978), 388.

"We were up against a solid wall" Barry D. Adam, *The Rise of a Gay and Lesbian Movement* (New York: Twayne Publishers, 1995), 46.

"Paris has always seemed" Linas Alsenas, *Gay America* (New York: Amulet Books, 2008), 34.

"You're neither unnatural" Erin McHugh, *Loud and Proud* (Los Angeles: Alyson Books, 2007), 121.

"I would rather give" David Leavitt, *The Man Who Knew Too Much* (New York: Atlas Books, 2006), 18.

"If You Are Gay" Charles Kaiser, *The Gay Metropolis* (New York: Grove Press, 1997), 19.

"At that time, $800" Eric Marcus, *Making Gay History* (New York: Harper Perennial, 2002), 29.

"At 9:30 am some" Lauritsen and Thorstad, *The Early Homosexual Rights Movement*, 40–42.

"I have resigned myself" Dose, *Magnus Hirschfeld*, 37.

Chapter 3

"Ask anyone who served" John Loughery, *The Other Side of Silence* (New York: John Macrae Books, 1998), 136.

"I stood there and he looked up" Alan Bérubé, *Coming Out Under Fire* (Chapel Hill: University of North Carolina Press, 1990), 197.

"[I] knew an awful lot" Ibid., 23.

"On behalf of the British government" Jim Burroway, "Today's Birthday: Alan Turing," Box Turtle Bulletin, June 23, 2014, www.boxturtlebulletin.com/2014/06/23/65287#1912.

"When we all walked in" Marcus, *Making Gay History*, 6.

"I venture to predict" Edythe Edye (Lisa Ben), "Here to Stay," *Vice Versa* 1, no. 4 (September 1947).

"I wanted to live it" Marcia M. Gallo, *Different Daughters* (New York: Carroll & Graf, 2006), xxxiv.

"Tolerance is the ugliest word" Donald Webster Cory, *The Homosexual in America* (New York: Greenberg, 1951), 151.

"[If an appeal were made] to the American traditions" Ibid., 243.

"Communists and queers" David K. Johnson, *The Lavender Scare* (Chicago: University of Chicago Press, 2004), 3.

"Homosexuals and other" George Chauncey, *Why Marriage?* (New York: Basic Books, 2004), 20.

"First, they are generally" Kaiser, *The Gay Metropolis*, 79–80.

"any criminal, infamous, dishonest" Johnson, *The Lavender Scare*, 123.

"exposing the pinks, the lavenders" Loughery, *The Other Side of Silence*, 199–204.

"Think of all the guys" *Hope Along the Wind* (Frameline, 2001), 00:35:42.

"We do not advocate" Lillian Faderman and Stuart Timmons, *Gay L.A.* (New York: Basic Books, 2006), 115.

"I'm tired of talking" Linda Hirshman, *Victory* (New York: Harper Perennial, 2012), 44.

"A mystic bond" Paul D. Cain, *Leading the Parade* (Lanham, MD: Scarecrow Press, 2002), 5.

"We weren't going to go out" Marcus, *Making Gay History*, 40.

"I have been miserable" Faderman and Timmons, *Gay L.A.*, 135.

"key positions with . . . the FBI" David F. Freeman, "How Much Do We Know About the Homosexual Male?", *ONE Magazine*, November 1955, 4–6.

"put up or shut up" Jim Burroway, "J. Edgar Hoover's Personal Interest in Gay Movements Revealed," Box Turtle Bulletin, September 25, 2013, www.boxturtlebulletin.com/2013/09/25/59187.

"no further action be taken" Jim Burroway, "FBI Launches Investigation Against *ONE Magazine*," Box Turtle Bulletin, January 26, 2014, www.boxturtlebulletin.com/2014/01/26.

"By winning this decision" Don Slater, "Victory! Supreme Court Upholds Homosexual Rights," *ONE Magazine*, February 1958, 17.

"We have let you see" Marcus, *Making Gay History*, 4.

"He replied that they could" Ibid., 5.

"Bronx GI Becomes a Woman" Christine Jorgensen, *Christine Jorgensen: A Personal Autobiography* (New York: Paul S. Eriksson, Inc., 1967), 138.

"All of America is anxiously awaiting" Ibid., 141.

"After a long talk" Ibid., 147–148.

"I thought for a moment" Ibid., 182.

"If I sneezed" Ibid., 188.

"Would you like to be" Gallo, *Different Daughters*, 1.

"[Bamberger] wanted it to be" Ibid., 1–2.

"gay girl of good moral character" Ibid., 4.

"Qui vive" Ibid., 5.

"I called up when I arrived" *Before Stonewall* (First Run Features, 1985), 00:47:51.

"It was a business meeting" Marcus, *Making Gay History*, 62.

"The movement was entirely run" Victoria A. Brownsworth, "Barbara Grier (1933–): Climbing the Ladder," in *Before Stonewall: Activists for Gay and Lesbian Rights in Historical Context*, ed. John Dececco and Vern L Bullough (New York: Routledge, 2002), 258.

"Thank you a thousand times over" Gallo, *Different Daughters*, 81–82.

"You never knew what" Rev. Troy D. Perry and Thomas L. P. Swicegood, *Profiles in Gay & Lesbian Courage* (New York: St. Martin's, 1991), 168.

"I decided that my dismissal" Marcus, *Making Gay History*, 81.

"For about eight months" Kaiser, *The Gay Metropolis*, 138–139.

"As an employer, the government's" Perry and Swicegood, *Profiles in Gay & Lesbian Courage*, 164.

"I am right and they are wrong" Hirshman, *Victory*, 58.

"God save us nelly queens" *Before Stonewall*, 01:09:42.

"I sang the song" Michael R. Gorman, *The Empress Is a Man* (New York: Harrington Park Press, 1998), 162.

"with the intent to deceive" Ibid., 179.

"The police knew a potential lawsuit" Ibid., 180.

"When are American homosexuals" William Lambert [Dorr Legg], "When Will Homosexuals Stop Pitying Themselves?", *ONE Magazine*, March 1959, 4–5.

"For those of us who were homosexual" *Before Stonewall*, 00:31:53.

Chapter 4

"I decided then" Jean M. White, "Those Others: A Report on Homosexuality," *Washington Post*, February 1, 1965.

"Applause for the challenger" Kay Tobin (Kay Lahusen), "'Expert' Challenged," *The Ladder* 9, nos. 5–6 (February–March 1965), 18.

"He was, let's say" Loughery, *The Other Side of Silence*, 250.

"I went down to City Hall" Gorman, *The Empress Is a Man*, 206.

"But that didn't stop me" Ibid., 207.

"My platform when I ran" Jim Burroway, "José Sarria Runs for San Francisco City Supervisor,"

Box Turtle Bulletin, November 7, 2013, www.boxturtlebulletin.com/2013/11/07/60044.

"I campaigned in schools" Gorman, *The Empress Is a Man*, 206–207.

"I lost the election" Cain, *Leading the Parade*, 40.

"Mr. Hoover would like to be" Marcus, *Making Gay History*, 91.

"9. Insist that you be treated" Jim Burroway, "FBI Collects Info on Homophile Groups 'Obstructing Efforts of the Bureau,'" Box Turtle Bulletin, June 4, 2014, www.boxturtlebulletin.com/2014/06/04/64955#1965.

"That's enough!" Marcus, *Making Gay History*, 101.

"It's useless to waste everybody's time" Alsenas, *Gay America*, 75.

"It is time that we begin to move" Frank Kameny, "Does Research into Homosexuality Matter?" *The Ladder* 9, no. 8 (May 1965), 14.

"Halt Government's War Against Homosexuals" Hirshman, *Victory*, 68.

"We had no idea" *Before Stonewall*, 01:13:11.

"It was thrilling" Marcus, *Making Gay History*, 105.

"I did not like parading around" *Stonewall Uprising* (American Experience, 2010), 00:43:50.

"a lot of guts to stand up" Gallo, *Different Daughters*, 115.

"If I had to specify" Kaiser, *The Gay Metropolis*, 147.

"It is time to open the closet door" Donn Teal, *The Gay Militants* (New York: St. Martin's, 1971), 62.

"Many of us who went south" *Before Stonewall*, 01:11:35.

"an immediate cessation" Susan Stryker, *Transgender History* (Berkeley, CA: Seal Press, 2008), 62.

"That's all the identification you need" Teal, *The Gay Militants*, 26.

"It's not against the law" Jim Burroway, "Flower Power Protest Against Los Angeles Police," Box Turtle Bulletin, August 17, 2014, www /boxturtlebulletin.com/2014/08/17/66518 #1968.

"I think these people are a fit subject" CBS Reports, *The Homosexuals* (3/7/67), 00:30:49.

"Instead of the homosexuals slinking off" David Carter, *Stonewall* (New York: St. Martin's, 2004), 147.

"Everybody's looking at each other" Marcus, *Making Gay History*, 127.

"Why don't you guys do something?!" Carter, *Stonewall*, 151.

"Flip the paddy wagon!" Hirshman, *Victory*, 98.

"I'll never forget the looks" Marcus, *Making Gay History*, 131.

"I had been in combat situations" Kaiser, *The Gay Metropolis*, 197.

"We are the Village girls!" Carter, *Stonewall*, 177.

"What's going on here?" Gallo, *Different Daughters*, 149–150.

"My father called and congratulated me" Hirshman, *Victory*, 101.

"We had discovered a power" *Stonewall Uprising*, 01:10:57.

"All of a sudden, I had brothers" Ibid., 01:14:40.

"It'll blow our cover" Perry Brass, "Sisters and Brothers: A Writer Hungering for Family Finds GLF," in *Smash the Church, Smash the State!*, ed. Tommi Avicolli Mecca (San Francisco: City Lights Books, 2009), 128.

Chapter 5

"You have to give them hope" James Daley, ed., *Great Speeches of Gay Rights* (Mineola, NY: Dover, 2010), 70.

"The Christopher Street Liberation Committee" Teal, *The Gay Militants*, 305.

"Out of the closets" *After Stonewall* (First Run Features, 1999), 00:12:11.

"For all of us who had" Robert Liechti, "Of the Day That Was and the Glory of It," *Gay Scene*, no. 3 (1970).

"You can't do that!" Teal, *The Gay Militants*, 14.

"They've lost that wounded look" Ibid., 7.

"We homosexuals plead with our people" *Stonewall Uprising*, 01:14:05.

"Let me tell you homosexuals" Fred W. McDarrah and Timothy S. McDarrah, *Gay Pride* (Chicago: A Cappella, 1994), 9.

"The time has come" Carter, *Stonewall*, 217.

"[It] became a community" Hirshman, *Victory*, 108.

"I was sitting with some friends" Marcus, *Making Gay History*, 141.

"It was like fire" Alsenas, *Gay America*, 90.

"Would you believe" Marcus, *Making Gay History*, 136.

"Every day brought something new" Néstor Latrónico, "My Memories as a Gay Militant in NYC," in Mecca, *Smash the Church, Smash the State!*, 49.

"[There] were all these gay people" *Vito* (First Run Features, 2011), 00:24:22.

"The experience of seeing those movies" Ibid., 00:24:35.

"It also seems like gay audiences" Michael Schiavi, *Celluloid Activist* (Madison: University of Wisconsin Press, 2011), 98.

"People were being taught" Marcus, *Making Gay History*, 141.

"I'm not missing a minute of this" Liz Highleyman, "Sylvia Rivera: A Woman Ahead of Her Time," in Mecca, *Smash the Church, Smash the State!*, 173.

"When we asked the community" Marcus, *Making Gay History*, 151.

"You people run if you want to" Stephen Cohen, *The Gay Liberation Youth Movement in New York* (New York: Routledge, 2007), 118.

"The idea was, these are like" Hirshman, *Victory*, 120–121.

"When are you going to speak" Carter, *Stonewall*, 243–244.

"I like to go on the rule of thumb" Teal, *The Gay Militants*, 213.

"wish homosexuality off" Schiavi, *Celluloid Activist*, 82–83.

"Good morning" Hirshman, *Victory*, 122–123.

"open channels to the gay community" Schiavi, *Celluloid Activist*, 84.

"Well, a rather interesting development" Edward Alwood, "Walter Cronkite and the Gay Rights Movement," *Washington Post*, July 26, 2009.

"a complete exchange of energy" Erin McHugh, *Homo History* (Los Angeles: Alyson Books, 2007), 112–113.

"the happiest check I ever wrote" Mark Segal, "New Book Reveals More on Gay Raiders' CBS News/Cronkite 'Zap'," *Philadelphia Gay News*, June 7, 2012.

"This is not a gimmick" Joyce Murdoch and Deb Price, *Courting Justice* (New York: Basic Books, 2001), 164.

"to permit two males to marry" Teal, *The Gay Militants*, 266.

"homosexual is after all" Murdoch and Price, *Courting Justice*, 165.

"lead to a breakdown" James T. Sears, *Rebels, Rubyfruit, and Rhinestones* (New Brunswick, NJ: Rutgers University Press, 2001), 59.

"it could spread" Eric Pianin, "Hearing Held on Women's Bid to Wed," *Louisville Times*, November 12, 1970.

"She is a woman" Sears, *Rebels, Rubyfruit, and Rhinestones*, 61.

"I am proud of my son" Jim Burroway, "I Am Proud of My Gay Son," Box Turtle Bulletin, April 29, 2014, www.boxturtlebulletin.com /2014/04/29/64234.

"Not everything happens in San Francisco" Jim Burroway, "First US Municipal Anti-Discrimination Ordinance," Box Turtle Bulletin, March 7, 2014, www.boxturtle bulletin.com/2014/03/07/63076.

"beat our people over the head" Hirshman, *Victory*, 132.

"I realized something" Ibid., 133.

"In those days gay psychiatrists" Kaiser, *The Gay Metropolis*, 236.

"Twenty Million Homosexuals Gain Instant Cure" Russell, *The Gay 100*, 290.

"There were so many men" Ellen Shumsky, "The Radicalesbian Story: An Evolution of Consciousness," in Mecca, *Smash the Church, Smash the State!*, 190.

"Enough already" Hirshman, *Victory*, 112–113.

"What is a lesbian?" Dudley Clendinen, *Out for Good* (New York: Touchstone, 1999), 91.

"Listen to her!" Schiavi, *Celluloid Activist*, 113.

"As a mother" Anita Bryant, *The Anita Bryant Story* (Ada, MI: Fleming H. Revell, 1977), 119.

"if gays are granted rights" McHugh, *Loud and Proud*, 10.

"Never Again, Never Forget" McDarrah and McDarrah, *Gay Pride*, 154.

"advocating, imposing, encouraging" Amy L. Stone, *Gay Rights on the Ballot Box* (Minneapolis: University of Minnesota Press, 2012), 14.

"Homosexuals want your children" Kaiser, *The Gay Metropolis*, 276.

"We had volunteers" *The Times of Harvey Milk* (Telling Pictures, 1984), 00:16:51.

"It was more than just" *The Times of Harvey Milk*, 00:18:06.

"You can stand around" Randy Shilts, *The Mayor of Castro Street* (New York: St. Martin's, 1982), 190.

"There was . . . pretty serious bashing" Jim Burroway, "Sydney Police Block Pride Parade," Box Turtle Bulletin, June 24, 2014, www.box turtlebulletin.com/2014/06/24/65303#1978.

"My name is Harvey Milk" Harvey Milk, *An Archive of Hope* (Oakland: University of California Press, 2013), 217.

"Come Out! Come Out!" Bronski, *A Queer History of the United States*, 220.

"Lesbian separatists worked with men" Faderman and Timmons, *Gay L.A.*, 214.

"Whatever else it is" Jim Burroway, "Prop 6/Briggs Initiative Defeated," Box Turtle

Bulletin, November 7, 2013, www.boxturtle
bulletin.com/2013/11/07/60044.

"To the gay community" *The Times of Harvey Milk*, 00:47:19.

"Most importantly, every gay person" *The Times of Harvey Milk*, 00:47:48.

"I think we sent a message" Ibid., 01:02:44.

"Good people, fine people" Ibid., 01:12:30.

"Harvey knew that the lowest nature" Perry and Swicegood, *Profiles in Gay & Lesbian Courage*, 19.

"Avenge Harvey Milk!" Steve Gdula, *Wearing History* (Los Angeles: Alyson Books, 2007), 54.

"If a bullet" Milk, *An Archive of Hope*, 246.

"I think it's time gay people" Perry and Swicegood, *Profiles in Gay & Lesbian Courage*, 119.

"For us the feeling" Marcus, *Making Gay History*, 230–231.

Chapter 6

"Doctors in New York" Lawrence K. Altman, "Rare Cancer Seen in 41 Homosexuals," *New York Times*, July 3, 1981.

"Like many others" Larry Kramer, *Reports from the Holocaust* (New York: St. Martin's, 1990), xxx.

"Eighty men sat down" Marcus, *Making Gay History*, 247.

"I hope you will write a check" Larry Kramer, "A Personal Appeal," *New York Native*, August 24–September 6, 1981.

"Question: Larry, does the president" Jim Burroway, "AIDS a Laughing Matter at the White House," Box Turtle Bulletin, October 15, 2013, www.boxturtlebulletin.com/2013/10/15/59615.

"There is no doubt" Kaiser, *The Gay Metropolis*, 285.

"People were acting" Marcus, *Making Gay History*, 269.

"If this article doesn't scare" Larry Kramer, "1,112 and Counting," *New York Native*, March 14–27, 1983.

"If we don't act" Ibid.

"It is necessary that we have a pool" Ibid.

"When straight nurses" Faderman and Timmons, *Gay L.A.*, 318.

"talking about how they'll never talk" *After Stonewall*, 00:44:24.

"Over 400 patients" Larry Kramer, "2,339 and Counting," *Village Voice*, October 4, 1983.

"I don't think that" Marcus, *Making Gay History*, 293.

"AIDS is not just God's punishment" McHugh, *Loud and Proud*, 31.

"the citizenry of this country" Alsenas, *Gay America*, 115–116.

"all AIDS carriers" William F. Buckley, "Crucial Steps in Combating the AIDS Epidemic; Identify All the Carriers," *New York Times*, March 18, 1986.

"tendency toward an intrinsic" Peter Freiberg, Rick Harding, and Mark Vandervelden, "The New Gay Activism: Adding Bite to the Movement," *The Advocate*, June 7, 1988.

"when civil legislation is introduced" Perry and Swicegood, *Profiles in Gay & Lesbian Courage*, 97–98.

"One of the saddest lessons" Larry Kramer, "Second-Rate Voice," *New York Native*, March 17, 1986.

"If we have somebody speaking" Marcus, *Making Gay History*, 272–273.

"Twenty years ago we marched" Perry and Swicegood, *Profiles in Gay & Lesbian Courage*, 94.

"We know we do not have" Ibid., 95.

"I remember a 12-year-old boy" Marcus, *Making Gay History*, 276.

"A good percentage of our kids" Ibid.

"Many people, especially our youth" Kaiser, *The Gay Metropolis*, 309.

"My position on AIDS" C. Everett Koop, MD, *Koop: Memoirs of America's Family Doctor* (New York: Random House, 1991), 216.

"We [had] to embarrass the administration" Kramer, *Reports from the Holocaust*, 136.

"to determine as soon as possible" Ibid., xiv.

"blood terrorists" Gdula, *Wearing History*, 102.

"because they know nothing" Ibid., 102.

"connection to blood" McHugh, *Homo History*, 117.

"firmly rooted in Judeo-Christian" Peter Irons, *The Courage of Their Convictions* (New York: Penguin, 1990), 390.

"This case is about" Dave Walter, "In The Justices' Own Words," *The Advocate*, August 5, 1986.

"1-2-3-4, civil rights or" Peter Freiberg, "Supreme Court Decision Sparks Protests: 'New Militancy' Seen in Angry Demonstrations," *The Advocate*, August 5, 1986.

"Every time they knock us down" David Walter, "High Court Upholds Sodomy Law," *The Advocate*, August 5, 1986.

"We have a message for Burger" Freiberg, "Supreme Court Decision," August 5, 1986.

"You've sold out the gay community!" Clendinen, *Out for Good*, 543.

"Turn on the lights" Marcus, *Making Gay History*, 292.

"Four years ago" Kramer, *Reports from the Holocaust*, 127.

"At the rate we are going" Ibid., 128.

"Every one of us here" Ibid., 136.

"At ACT UP I found" Marcus, *Making Gay History*, 307.

"It [was] like living in a war" *How to Survive a Plague* (Sundance Selects, 2012), 00:08:01.

"I said, 'Enough of this'" Ibid., 00:11:55.

"You guys don't know diddly" Ibid., 00:15:05.

"It was like . . . lotus flower" *We Were Here* (Docurama Films, 2012), 01:16:01.

"I didn't understand what it was" Cain, *Leading the Parade*, 279.

"After a little while" Jim Burroway, "ACT UP Occupies the FDA," Box Turtle Bulletin, October 11, 2013, www.boxturtlebulletin.com/2013/10/11/59558.

"It sort of felt like reaching" *How to Survive a Plague*, 00:34:21.

"Stop killing us" Chris Bull and John Gallagher, *Perfect Enemies* (New York: Crown, 1996), 76.

"As long as the epidemic" Mark Blasius and Shane Phelan, eds., "ACT UP Post-Action Position Statement, 1989," *We Are Everywhere* (New York: Routledge, 1997), 626.

"Surely ACT UP has taught everyone" Kramer, *Reports from the Holocaust*, 289.

"Not only has the AIDS epidemic" Larry Kramer, letter to the editor, *The Nation*, March 20, 1989.

Chapter 7

"Come out and face the people!" Daniel M. Weintraub and Scott Harris, "Gay Rights Protest Disrupts Wilson Speech," *Los Angeles Times*, October 2, 1991.

"There is a religious war" Patrick J. Buchanan, "1992 Republican National Convention Speech," August 17, 1992, Patrick J. Buchanan official website, http://buchanan.org/blog/1992-republican-national-convention-speech-148.

"Family Rights Forever" Bull and Gallagher, *Perfect Enemies*, 88.

"Americans try to raise their children" Ibid., 94.

"We find nothing special" Romer v. Evans, 517 U.S. 620 (1996).

"You don't need to be 'straight'" Robert Goldberg, *Barry Goldwater* (New Haven: Yale University Press, 1997), 332.

"When a president takes on tough issues" Bull and Gallagher, *Perfect Enemies*, 157.

"promote homosexuality or" Michelle Baker and Stephen Tropiano, *Queer Facts* (London: Arcane, 2004), 42.

"It was wrongly assumed" McHugh, *Loud and Proud*, 99.

"How could we say that men" Jim Burroway, "Today's Birthdays: Simon Tseko Nkoli," Box Turtle Bulletin, November 26, 2013, www.boxturtlebulletin.com/2013/11/26/60659.

"I have no doubt" Parkinson, *A Little Gay History*, 92.

"Be aware of the changing" Bull and Gallagher, *Perfect Enemies*, 219.

"We will not accept two people" Ibid., 220.

"as big a lie as any" Steven Lee Myers, "How a 'Rainbow Curriculum' Turned into Fighting Words," *New York Times*, December 13, 1992.

"We have no books" Betsy Bird, Julie Danielson, and Peter Sieruta, *Wild Things!* (Somerville, MA: Candlewick Press), 124.

"I would not be standing here" Chauncey, *Why Marriage?*, 53.

"It was like watching a no-hitter" *We Were Here*, 01:19:32.

"Someday the AIDS crisis" Vito Russo, *Out Spoken, Reel Two* (New York: White Crane Books, 2012), 283–284.

"This tragedy—it taught us" *We Were Here*, 01:24:17.

"The basis of this club" *Out of the Past* (Allumination, 1997), 00:39:01.

"Bad enough that they" Evan Wolfson, *Why Marriage Matters* (New York: Simon & Schuster, 2004), 34.

"Their commitment, their love" *No Secret Anymore* (Frameline, 2010), 00:53:14.

"I felt lucky to play" Brandon Voss, "Ryan Phillippe: Cool Intentions," *The Advocate*, May 12, 2010.

"Adult content?" Marcus, *Making Gay History*, 397.

"It didn't matter if" Ibid., 373.

"Go home, give your kids" Moisés Kaufman, *The Laramie Project* (New York: Vintage, 2001), 70.

"The idea was to keep Phelps" Marcus, *Making Gay History*, 415.

"Phelps had arrived" Ibid., 416.

"I would like nothing better" Kaufman, *The Laramie Project*, 96.

"altercation between soldiers" Alsenas, *Gay America*, 139.

"I want to thank Brandon Teena" Hilary Swank, Academy Award acceptance speech, transcript,
March 26, 2000, http://aaspeechesdb.oscars.org/link/072-3/.

"I can't bring [Matthew] back" Hirshman, *Victory*, 277.

"a hate crime against parents" Gdula, *Wearing History*, 170.

"Boy Scouts was community" Chuck Sudetic, "The Struggle for the Soul of the Boy Scouts," *Rolling Stone*, July 6–10, 2000.

"The only apparent explanation" Jan Crawford Greenburg, "Scouts Can Ban Gay Leader in N.J. Discrimination Case," *Chicago Tribune*, June 29, 2000.

Chapter 8

"Indeed, Miss Manners" McHugh, *Loud and Proud*, 98.

"I really believe that the pagans" Jim Burroway, "Jerry Falwell Blames Gays for 9/11," Box Turtle Bulletin, September 13, 2013, www.boxturtlebulletin.com/2013/09/13/58961.

"to prohibit certain immoral conduct" Carlos A. Ball, *From the Closet to the Courtroom* (Boston: Beacon Press, 2010), 231.

"Bowers was not correct" Lawrence v. Texas, 539 U.S. 558 (2003).

"Many Americans do not want" *Lawrence v. Texas*.

"the core concept" *Lawrence v. Texas*.

"The Massachusetts Constitution affirms" Chauncey, *Why Marriage?*, 134–135.

"The freedom to marry has" Loving v. Virginia, 388 U.S. 1 (1967).

"I am still not a political person" Mildred Loving, "Loving for All, Public Statement on the 40th Anniversary of *Loving v. Virginia*," June 12, 2007.

"I was disgusted" Jonah Owen Lamb, "Gavin Newsom Has No Regrets About Leading Same-Sex Marriage Charge," *San Francisco Examiner*, February 10, 2014.

"I acted in order to honor" Amy Rennert, ed., *We Do* (San Francisco: Chronicle Books, 2004), 6.

"We thought they'd be" Lamb, "Gavin Newsom," February 10, 2014.

"A volunteer approached us" Rennert, *We Do*, 73.

"the happiest place on earth" Ibid., 95.

"Del is 83 years old" Jim Burroway, "Today's Birthdays: Phyllis Lyon," Box Turtle Bulletin, November 10, 2013, www.boxturtlebulletin.com/2013/11/10/60258.

"After more than two centuries" "Transcript of Bush Statement," CNN.com, February 24, 2004, www.cnn.com/2004/ALLPOLITICS/02/24/elec04.prez.bush.transcript/.

"Will you marry me" Reid Foregrave, "Pair Reflects on Months as Married Gay Couple," *Des Moines Register*, January 20, 2008.

"When all is said and done" Chad Nation, "Iowa Supreme Court: Gay Marriage Ban Illegal," *Southwest Iowa News*, April 3, 2009.

"Guess what I learned" Stone, *Gay Rights on the Ballot Box*, 36.

"Apology accepted" Jim Burroway, "Frank Kameny Fired from Government Job for Being Gay," Box Turtle Bulletin, December 20, 2013, www.boxturtlebulletin.com/2013/12/20/61157.

"It's in the Internet" David Boies and Theodore B. Olson, *Redeeming the Dream* (New York: Viking, 2014), 147.

"I believe that adopting" Ibid., 157.

"My heart breaks" Dan Savage and Terry Miller, *It Gets Better* (New York: Plume, 2012), 2.

"Why are we waiting for permission" Jim Burroway, "Dan Savage," Box Turtle Bulletin, October 7, 2014, www.boxturtlebulletin.com/2014/10/07/67277#1964b.

"Gay rights are human rights" Parkinson, *A Little Gay History*, 22.

"I pledge to lead" "Take the Athlete Ally Pledge," Athlete Ally, www.athleteally.org/action/athlete-ally-pledge/.

"I am absolutely comfortable" Joe Biden, interview by David Gregory, *Meet the Press*, NBC, May 6, 2012.

"At a certain point" Phil Gast, "Obama Announces He Supports Same-Sex Marriage," CNN.com, May 9, 2012, www.cnn.com/2012/05/09/politics/obama-same-sex-marriage/.

"The president, I think" Ibid.

"I [didn't] wanna be" *Edie & Thea* (QC Cinema, 2009), 00:33:58.

"DOMA undermines both the public" United States v. Windsor, 570 U.S. ___ (2013).

"As far as this Court is concerned" *United States v. Windsor.*

"We are a better people" Whitewood v. Wolf, 992 Supp. 2d 410.

"No union is more profound" Obergefell v. Hodges, 576 U.S. ___ (2015).

Afterword

"Never doubt that a small group" McHugh, *Loud and Proud*, 12.

"Our children want us to be married" Theresa Volpe, "Testimony of Mercedes Santos and Theresa Volpe Before the Illinois Senate Executive Committee," January 2, 2013, Lambda Legal, www.lambdalegal.org/in-court/legal-docs/leg_il_20130102_testimony-santos-volpe-hb5170.

All other quotes, interview with Theresa Volpe and Mercedes Santos, November 21, 2014.

▲ ▼ ▲

Index

Page numbers in *italics* indicate pictures.

▲ ▼ ▲